Praise for W

"*I simply <u>love</u> this book. Eldon writes in a brilliant, thought-provoking style, challenging and encouraging us to be fully present to our life's journey.*"

— **Colette Baron-Reid**, internationally renowned intuitive counselor and the best-selling author of *Messages from Spirit* and *The Map*

"*Few are the authors who turn you inside out, who blow up your preconceived notions and cause you to become honest with yourself through and through. That's precisely what happens when you read **What If?** I highly recommend this book to those spiritual warriors who are unflinching in their journey to the Authentic Self.*"

— **Dr. Michael Bernard Beckwith**, the author of *Spiritual Liberation: Fulfilling Your Soul's Potential*

"*If, like Neo in the film **The Matrix**, you are ready to swallow the red pill, then consume Eldon Taylor's book **What If? The Challenge of Self-Realization** and wake up in a new reality where you'll discover truth instead of illusion. Eldon will first show you how you dance at the end of a web of strings like a mindless puppet. The strings are attached to us by whatever we're attached to. They're connected to us through our culture, beliefs, needs, wants and desires— by habit and by fear. Or—your choice—you can continue to take the blue pills, leave the book on the shelf, and the opportunity ends. Nothing will change. Life will go on as usual and you can believe whatever you want to believe.*"

— **Thomas Campbell**, Department of Defense and NASA consultant, physicist, and the author of *My Big TOE*

"*What a perfect follow-up to Eldon's last three best-selling books—I love it! Rather than trying to convince you of the validity of thought control, Eldon peels back the layers of your own mind and helps you separate yourself and your beliefs from those foisted upon you by society. If you truly wish to do more than just give lip service to personal empowerment, this book is a must!*"

— **Peggy McColl**, the *New York Times* best-selling author of *Your Destiny Switch*

"*If you're a spiritual seeker ready to stretch beyond your comfort zone and throw out everything you think you already know, read this book. The scenarios and questions posed by Eldon Taylor in this courageous work will have your mind spinning with deliberation, punctuated with periods of self-righteousness and maybe even indignation. You've entered the twilight zone; and if you don't squirm even a little, I'd be surprised. As Dr. Taylor points out early on, this book isn't for the 'faint of heart.' For some, the question 'What if . . . ?' will be too painful to contemplate. For select others, however, it will be an awakening of the Spirit, an opportunity to fully experience our world of uncertainty and contradictions . . . and be at peace with it.*"

— **Dr. Karen Kan**, Law of Attraction relationship author and coach

"*A must-read mind-bender,* **What If?** *is a thought-provoking and enjoyable read. Prepare to be awakened to truth as Dr. Taylor leads you on a journey of self-discovery. By shining light on false assumptions for a revealing look beneath the surface appearance of things,* **What If?** *is a primer for evolving your consciousness and mastering your mind. The book is both a remarkable achievement and a valuable contribution at this time in human history when so much is at stake!*"

— **K. G. Stiles**, author, therapist, and director of Health Mastery Systems and **PurePlantEssentials.com**

"With characteristic insight, Eldon Taylor brilliantly examines some of the fundamental issues of our existence: spirituality, power, human rights, free will, and morality. By using Socratic questioning, he challenges readers to inquire more deeply into the murky gray areas of their lives. After artfully presenting this multidimensional overview of the human condition, he then provides us with specific ways to transform our experience of both the world in general and of ourselves in particular. Uplifting, readable, and highly recommended."

— **Chuck Hillig**, the author of *Enlightenment for Beginners, Seeds for the Soul, Looking for God: Seeing the Whole in One, The Way IT Is,* and *The Magic King*

"Eldon Taylor goes to the root of the turmoil, chaos, conflict, fear, and stress we see in the world today. In effect, we've devolved into a 'dumbed-down' society, one disconnected from reality—one in which the gap between who we think we are and who we really are seems to be widening all the time. He masterfully examines the causes of this gap by discussing some of life's most difficult issues and concerns, then asking 'What if?' in the hopes that the reader will be able to put things in perspective and close the reality gap."

— **Michael E. Tymn**, journalist, author, and vice-president of the Academy of Spirituality and Paranormal Studies

"In keeping with his theme of progressive awareness, in **What If?** Eldon Taylor poses questions that force us to examine our inner being. In this wonderful book, Eldon allows the reader to provide answers that may be quite surprising—even shocking—as one's true nature comes forth. I highly recommend this book as a step toward enlightenment. Read it and read it again. I followed the instructions, putting the book down for a time after each chapter. I believe my second reading of the book will generate even more thoughts as days, months, or years from now, my outlook may change in interesting ways. It's said that if a man thinks now as he did ten years before, then he has wasted ten years. To read the book after some time has passed will be interesting. I suspect it's a volume that one can read again and again and extract a different meaning each time— somewhat like Musashi's **The Book of Five Rings**."

— **Dr. John L. Turner**, the author of
Medicine, Miracles & Manifestations

"**What If?** is thought-provoking and much more. The book offers an emotional and spiritual journey into self-discovery. Each chapter serves as a catalyst for personal growth. With his usual ease, depth, and creative style, Eldon Taylor explores current as well as timeless topics. No doubt readers will encounter the ultimate—themselves."

— **Dianne Arcangel, M.S.**,
the author of *Afterlife Encounters*

"*Eldon invites self-realization,*
Dispelling programmed expectation
How to process the data stream
And still live out your American dream . . .
Read this book . . . dispel illusions . . .
And lovingly come to your own conclusions."

— **Shelley Stockwell-Nicholas, Ph.D.**, president of the International Hypnosis Federation and the author of *The Search for Cosmic Consciousness*

"*Another slam dunk for Eldon Taylor. That most elusive of subjects, the Self, is tackled brilliantly and thoughtfully by one of the master thinkers of our time.* **What If? The Challenge of Self-Realization** *covers concepts like traveling through thought (not time) with a deep examination of humanity and the quest for common human values. By the way, any mentor named SPA gets my attention! Eldon has* a surprise chapter with treats to delight your mind in a book that brought both tears to my eyes and hope to my heart."

— **Terri Marie**, CEO, White Wing Entertainment

"More than another brain trigger, **What If?** is a deeply stirring soul trigger. Eldon Taylor never fails to compel his readers to question reality and the role they play in their perception of it. The very best educator is one who inspires his students to think things through for themselves!"

— **Angelina Heart**, the author of
The Teaching of Little Crow: The Journey of the Soul

"Eldon Taylor continues his exploration into subtle—yet inherently fundamental—processes native to humans with a thinking brain, whose emotions drive behavior at all levels of the human condition. This is especially relevant when living in community with others who are prone to the same challenging dilemma. This book is an insightful, provocative view of how conscious decision making includes perceptions, emotions, and choices, and how we think, how we act, and how we experience life in its multiple expressions. To know oneself is the greatest challenge of the life experience because self-evaluation is a moment-to-moment thought experiment."

— **Elaine Smitha**, the author of
If You Make The Rules, How Come You're Not Boss?;
producer and host, Evolving Ideas© Radio & TV

"Who knows how much of our own mind really belongs to us? How much of the way we think is governed by the outside programming of popular media, family dynamics, or deeply embedded cultural and historical influences? Eldon Taylor's new book **What If?** peels back the layers of our own thinking to reveal our authentic selves, or conversely, *the product of someone else's programming. This provocative book helps us look at all the What-ifs in our own lives."*

— **Caroline Sutherland,** the author of
The Body Knows . . . How to Stay Young

"Thought-provoking, insightful, fascinating, irreverent and challenging are just a few words to describe Eldon Taylor's **What If?** *This guide to finding your authentic self will have you question your assumptions, think outside the box, and grow personally and spiritually; and it will provide you with the ability to better understand yourself and come closer to achieving enlightenment. I recommend it most highly for everyone wishing to break through limiting beliefs, put an end to resignation and apathy, and be fully challenged so as to achieve greater happiness and fulfillment."*

— **Dr. Joe Rubino,** founder of
CenterForPersonalReinvention.com;
creator, **SelfEsteemSystem.com**

"Self-realization is your ticket to wholeness, joy, personal freedom, health . . . even wealth. Eldon Taylor's books, CDs, and other products are always cutting edge. I highly recommend his latest pearls of wisdom."

— **Doris Helge, Ph.D.,** the author of *Joy on the Job*

"Eldon Taylor has broken the mold of most self-help writers as he tackles head-on many taboo questions. Bold, forthright, and most certainly profound, **What If? The Challenge of Self-Realization** *takes the reader on a number of thought experiments to expose how much of our power we've given away. The lessons in this book are vital if you wish to experience what it is to be free to reach your highest level of self-actualization."*

— **Dr. Nick Begich,** the author of
Controlling the Human Mind

"*Personal empowerment just took a quantum leap in this astonishing book by Eldon Taylor. **What If? The Challenge of Self-Realization** consists of a series of thought experiments that will move you out of the rigid beliefs you didn't even know you had, into a way of life that allows you to fully express your amazing uniqueness and gifts. I highly recommend it.*"

— **Crystal Andrus**, the best-selling author of
Simply . . . Woman! and *Simply . . . EMPOWERED!*

"*Give this man a pen and paper, and out comes a masterpiece. Eldon Taylor has done it again! He covers every corner of spirituality and then takes it out of the box for all to comprehend. Chapter 13 is a mind stopper. It gives the reader a chance to quiet the mind and understand the pursuit of happiness and peace with integrity.*"

— **Hossca Harrison**, founder of *Jonah Life Institute*

"*Dr. Taylor's new book, **What If? The Challenge of Self-Realization**, is a must-read for all those who are learning to read outside the box. It's one of his most insightful and provocative books yet. I highly recommend it.*"

— **Peter Calhoun**, the author of *Soul on Fire*

"*In the latest in his books exploring vital issues relating to believing versus knowing, Eldon Taylor engages readers in thoughtful and thought-provoking questions designed to help us discover who we really are. He guides us to look at ourselves, our actions, and our values through fresh eyes. The implications for our society are far-reaching. **What If?** is a book that deserves to be read and discussed by friends, families, and groups throughout our country.*"

— **Steven Halpern**, composer, recording artist,
and the author of *Sound Health*

*"After his books **Choices and Illusions, Mind Programming** and **What Does That Mean?**, there's one word that
came to my mind in defining Eldon Taylor's style, which I
noticed in this latest book also: <u>magnetic.</u> Once I started to
read, I couldn't let the books out of my hands until I finished
them. As with his previous works, **What If?** is written for
all those already in the fast lane who desire to accelerate their
spiritual growth, as well as for those just beginning their
spiritual journey. Designed as a remarkably dynamic inner
dialogue, the book continually challenges readers to always be
aware of all possible motivations behind their choices. When
a decision to act is made, it should be done from the highest
level of consciousness. Through numerous examples of refin-
ing choice analysis, readers are offered a gift of learning—an
invaluable life skill. We're ultimately invited to look inward
with honesty, detachment, and an open mind; and to start the
process of re-creating ourselves with wisdom while being aware
of all the subtleties of the subconscious mind. The ultimate
goal is the re-creation of the real self, free from imperfections
induced by the illusions of this life. Knowing that this is a long
process, we have to learn patience and develop consistency.
With each book, continuing to offer us the tools for self-
realization, Eldon Taylor proves again to be a great teacher.
His contribution to the continual empowerment of the human
race on its way to spiritual ascension cannot be disputed."*

— **Cristian Enescu, M.D.**

*"Being truly awake to yourself, to higher potential, and
to the world around you may require an unraveling from
what you think you know and believe about yourself, right
and wrong, and true and false. Once again, Eldon Taylor
takes us on a journey of deep (not always easy) reflections
that reveal the vast inconsistencies of our own beliefs, values, and perspectives—and the conditioning that shapes
the reality they appear to have created. A worthy, albeit at
times uncomfortable exploration, **What If?** will offer you
profound insights, not through answers or advice from an*

authority, but by inviting you to explore various scenarios and questions that don't always come with easy, clear answers. This book will help you access an intelligence that exists beyond the conclusions, assessments, opinions, and judgments that have conditioned you to believe things you don't really agree with; and in the process, you'll wake up to a more authentic you!"

— **Anita Pathik Law,** the author of *The Power of Our Way: A Path to a Collective Consciousness* and *Returning to Your Original Intention: Embracing Your Own Becoming*

"This book should come with a warning. It's a black belt in how to discover your true essence. It turned me inside out and chopped me on the head! Don't get this book unless you're really willing to find yourself where you can't believe you are. **What If? The Challenge of Self-Realization** is too soft a title for this book. Reading it is living it, and you must prepare yourself for the challenge."

— **Shazzie,** ecstatic being, visionary in paradise, author, artist, mother, loveworker

"In a world where governments, corporations, and religious institutions compete to capture our attention and then mold our thoughts about ourselves, Eldon's keen insight into this struggle is a valuable asset for anyone desiring to rise above the fray and regain control of their own mind. The power to be confident and comfortable with oneself as an individual without blaming others brings great freedom. Well done."

— **JZ Knight,** author of the best-selling autobiography *A State of Mind: My Story*

What If?

ALSO BY ELDON TAYLOR

Change Without Thinking (DVD)*

*Choices and Illusions: How Did I Get Where I Am, and How Do I Get Where I Want to Be?**

Exclusively Fabricated Illusions

I Believe: When What You Believe Matters

Just Be: A Little Cowboy Philosophy

Little Black Book

*Mind Programming: From Persuasion and Brainwashing to Self-Help and Practical Metaphysics**

Simple Things and Simple Thoughts

Subliminal Communication: Emperor's Clothes or Panacea?

Subliminal Learning: An Eclectic Approach

Subliminal Technology: Unlocking the Power of Your Own Mind

Thinking Without Thinking: Who's in Control of Your Mind?

Wellness: Just a State of Mind

*What Does That Mean? Exploring Mind, Meaning, and Mysteries**

Plus hundreds of audio and video programs in multiple languages.

*Available from Hay House

Please visit:
Hay House USA: **www.hayhouse.com**®
Hay House Australia: **www.hayhouse.com.au**
Hay House UK: **www.hayhouse.co.uk**
Hay House South Africa: **www.hayhouse.co.za**
Hay House India: **www.hayhouse.co.in**

What If?

The Challenge
of Self-Realization

ELDON TAYLOR

HAY HOUSE, INC.
Carlsbad, California • New York City
London • Sydney • Johannesburg
Vancouver • Hong Kong • New Delhi

Published and distributed in the United States by: Hay House, Inc.:
www.hayhouse.com • *Published and distributed in Australia by:*
Hay House Australia Pty. Ltd.: www.hayhouse.com.au • *Published
and distributed in the United Kingdom by:* Hay House UK, Ltd.:
www.hayhouse.co.uk • *Published and distributed in the Republic
of South Africa by:* Hay House SA (Pty), Ltd.: www.hayhouse.co.za
• *Distributed in Canada by:* Raincoast: www.raincoast.com • *Published in India by:* Hay House Publishers India: www.hayhouse.co.in

Editorial supervision: Jill Kramer
Edited by: Suzanne Brady and Ravinder Taylor
Project editor: Jessica Kelley • *Design:* Riann Bender

Library of Congress Cataloging-in-Publication Data

Taylor, Eldon.
  What if? : the challenge of self-realization / Eldon Taylor. -- 1st ed.
    p. cm.
  ISBN 978-1-4019-2737-0 (hbk. : alk. paper) 1. Self-realization. 2.
Self (Philosophy) 3. Self-perception. 4. Self-knowledge, Theory of.
I. Title.
  BJ1470.T39 2011
  158.1--dc22

                                        2010032880

Tradepaper ISBN: 978-1-4019-2738-7
Digital ISBN: 978-1-4019-3087-5

15 14 13 12   5 4 3 2
1st edition, March 2011
2nd edition, June 2012

Printed in the United States of America

❖❖❖

*To the wonder and genuine mystery
of life and to all of you who together
are inseparable from the mystery.*

❖❖❖

Contents

"'The unknown,' said Faxe's soft voice in the forest, 'the unforetold, the unproven, that is what life is based on. Ignorance is the ground of thought. Unproof is the ground of action. If it were proven that there is no God there would be no religion. No Handdara, no Yomesh, no hearthgods, nothing. But also if it were proven that there is a God, there would be no religion. . . . Tell me, Genry, what is known? What is sure, predictable, inevitable—the one certain thing you know concerning your future, and mine?'

"'That we shall die.'

"'Yes. There's really only one question that can be answered, Genry, and we already know the answer. . . . The only thing that makes life possible is permanent, intolerable uncertainty; not knowing what comes next.'"

— URSULA K. LeGUIN, *THE LEFT HAND OF DARKNESS*

Preface

For years I have studied the human mind—how it works, why it betrays us, the effect it has on our bodies, and so forth. Most of my earlier work deals directly with this, and I believe that in the past I've made a very strong case for why we must take control of our thoughts. Our natural psychology, our desire to be loved, accepted, stimulated, and excited, makes it easy for others to manipulate us. Whether it occurs organically, such as in peer pressure or codependent patterns, or it happens deliberately, such as in the advertising and entertainment industries and even in government conspiracies, our thoughts are being manipulated on an almost 24/7 basis.

However, it's one thing to learn about the extremes others are going to in order to control you and quite another to look directly at your own thoughts and realize that they make no sense, that you're holding two opposing views at the same time and were totally unaware of it, that you actually disagree (and disagree strongly, at that) with your own beliefs. This is why my books and other writings have taken what seems to be a new course.

It's my hope that once you've finished this book, you will have had enough "in your face" encounters with yourself that you'll truly be able to examine your life, beliefs, and values anew, for it's only by doing this that I believe you can begin the journey of discovering who you really are.

One last item—I suggest that you read this book one chapter at a time. I mean by that: read a chapter and pause. Put the book down and think about the material before rushing on. The content in this book often reveals itself one layer at a time, or so others have informed me.

Introduction

Not Time Travelers
but Thought Travelers

". . . the quest for certainty blocks the search for meaning. Uncertainty is the very condition to impel man to unfold his powers."

— ERICH FROMM

What if you awoke tomorrow and had no idea who you were? What if you discovered that you were not at all who you thought you were? What if you'd invested your life in a belief only to find out it was totally false? What if you were given a chance to change and you refused, only to discover that the change would have made all the difference? What if you *did* change and then learned you'd been right beforehand? What if you discovered there was no right or wrong at all?

The true challenge of self-realization is in discovering the authentic self. People typically believe they know who they are when indeed they don't. That may sound preposterous, but by the time you've read this book, I'm certain you'll be questioning exactly what it is that defines you.

This work is all about peeling back layers. In our desire to be accepted, we frequently choose to follow the crowd and thereby accept the inconsistencies contained in the assumptions and convictions that are handed to us in the process.

This book is about looking squarely at who we are through fresh eyes. Self-actualization begins by finding *who* it is that we seek to actualize. Each chapter is designed to assist in that discovery. Sometimes the best way to learn what something is, is first to eliminate what it is not. We'll use much of this approach in the pages that follow.

We'll also explore the notion of *reductio ad absurdum,* a form of argument in which a proposition is disproven by following its implications to a logical but absurd consequence.

Thought Travelers

To facilitate the mission of finding the authentic self, I've chosen to make a thought traveler out of you. By using your imagination to explore different scenarios, you'll travel in time and take on other personalities. The objective is to make the process somewhat experiential. In this way, I believe it may be possible to open yourself up to a deeper level of understanding, perhaps an epiphany—or even better, a greater degree of enlightenment. Additionally, I've decided to include matters that it's all too likely you were taught to avoid. They come under the labels of religion and politics, and you may find the discussions uncomfortable or even offensive. I'll ask several questions about these subjects, including: *Do you need to be involved in order to grow spiritually?*

I believe that our participation in the world is our work. It's written in the Bible: "You will know them by their fruits [work]." We are either directly participating or indirectly giving consent just by tacitly allowing things to happen. Consent to what? That's definitely a part of what we'll look at.

This is just a primer, for it would be impossible to cover all of the questions that could be asked. However, the process is designed to develop within you an earnest desire to seek the answers that will lead to your experiencing what is meant by the directive: *Know thyself.* You can't know yourself if you live on automatic pilot, tacitly consenting with no awareness of what you're agreeing to, in a democracy without a voice, in a world with your eyes closed or so closely focused that you can't see what's going on right in front of you.

Who Am I?

As humans, we like to think that we're in control—at least somewhat. We like to feel that there's some certainty that makes our lives predictable. We go to bed and expect to awaken. Further, we expect that when we wake up, we'll still be in the same bed. We look in the mirror and expect that the face looking back at us will be the same familiar face that has always been there. Even as we age, we expect the process to be gradual, and therefore we won't suddenly be bald or have white hair or skin that droops. We expect that the sun will rise again tomorrow and that the people we know will still be the same as they always have been. We imagine many things but seldom give thought to the real precariousness of our lives. Perhaps that's due in part to our fear of uncertainty—fear of loss, of the end, that we'll cease and be no more.

Within most—if not all—of us is a potential to express what has been called "the Lucifer effect," doing terrible things to innocent people.[1] Behavioral science has repeatedly demonstrated that not only does this exist, but so does the potential for denial. So those who would either commit an evil act or fail to do something about awful events they witness will vociferously deny that they would ever behave that way.

Is it fair to say we're certain about our uncertainty, or is it more appropriate to say we're uncertain about our certainty? Does it matter? For me, the answer is an emphatic yes, because everything I do, everything I believe, everything I invest my life energy into is, in one way or another, the expression of who I am or can become. Can I then be certain of anything?

What Do I Know?

What do you say you know? How do you know it? Is it an absolute epistemological certainty?

You can't truly know yourself without peeling back the layers that are the result of your enculturation, the propaganda you've swallowed as literal and real, the subconscious strategies that are hidden from you and designed to protect you from rejection, pain, and the like. In short, you must persevere in order to endure a thorough and honest evaluation of your beliefs and ideals. As such, this book is not for the fainthearted, as it isn't designed just to make you *feel good*. I tackle a number of taboo subjects, such as politics and religion, and some of the thought experiments I ask you to participate in are simply unpleasant.

I guarantee there will be at least one section of this book that will upset you. You may even be tempted to stop reading in disgust. However, if you truly wish to discover who you are and to begin the journey to enlightenment, then you must be prepared to face yourself honestly. I only ask you not to jump to conclusions too soon. I don't intend to take a position on any of the issues. Rather, I try to expose all sides, and sometimes this is done through the lens of the opposition.

It has been my experience, and my research has often borne out this observation, that many people are simply "asleep." By this I mean unaware of just how automatic and unconscious everything they are has become. *Knee-jerk, reflexive, reactive,* and similar terms describe the way that many people live. It's no wonder that it's so common for them to come to that point in life where they seriously ask, "Is that all there is?" These are the individuals who put bumper stickers on their cars with sayings such as: "Thank God it's Friday," "Life sucks and then you die," "Go ahead—make my day," "I don't get even—I get evener," and so on.

If you're one of those people, I don't mean to demean or insult you, but you have to know that you're not reaching your highest potential, and I seriously doubt that you're genuinely happy. I've dedicated much of my work to assisting those who desire to find their authentic selves and live accordingly. To that end, I welcome you to a journey that promises to take you deeply into the possibility that everything you believe just may be wrong—and to help you ask the persistent question: *What does that mean?*

What would it mean to you if you discovered that everything you believed was wrong—and if not everything, then much of it? What then? How much of your life is dictated by beliefs that—if they were false—would dramatically change your life?

I've asked these questions of many, and some have answered, "Not much." How about you? I believe it's important that you discover these answers yourself, for if I were to give you *my* answers, then you would be no closer to finding your own true or authentic self. Let's just see. May you enjoy the adventure.

chapter 1

Preparing for the Journey

"Knowledge is an unending adventure at the edge of uncertainty."

— JACOB BRONOWSKI

Your adventure begins with a close look at how you might acquire some, if not all, of your beliefs. I could ask: *Are you hypnotized?*

Let's consider an idea suggested by Richard Bach in his book *Hypnotizing Maria.*[1] Imagine that a stage hypnotist has hypnotized you. The experience will seem quite real, even if it's a pure hallucination, whether negative or positive in nature. (A negative hallucination occurs when you fail to see what's there, and a positive one is when you see what *isn't* there.) Imagine you've been imprisoned in a room without doors. The structure is made of solid concrete, like a bomb shelter or bunker; and the walls, floor, and ceiling are several feet thick. You're trapped inside without exits.

Think about this for a moment. Perhaps you circle the stage, walking around the room that only you can see. The audience has been told that you believe you're trapped in a solid concrete room. You touch the cold walls when the hypnotist suggests that you try to find a way out. You push on them and find that they aren't just cold and hard, but their surface is rough like a sidewalk. You kick the wall and hurt your foot. When prompted by the hypnotist, you search for seams and find none. You begin to worry—how will you get out? What if the light disappears? Where is the light coming from? Fear crawls over you.

Now imagine that you're in the audience instead. You're witnessing a hypnotized individual trapped in an imaginary room. That is, the barrier he perceives as a concrete wall doesn't actually exist. The walled-in subject is trapped only by his beliefs. From your perspective as an observer, it seems almost ridiculous that this self-imposed idea, this hallucination, this state of mind in hypnosis, could possibly be real. You laugh at the person as he becomes frantic to escape. His antics grow increasingly panicked, and you laugh louder and harder.

Self-Imposed Limitations

Now imagine that you're living in a world of your own self-imposed limitations and that you're doing so right now—this very minute, as you're reading this book. How many of these self-created walls have you been hypnotized into believing are real? Isn't that what accepting a suggestion is—a state of hypnosis? How many ideas have you accepted from the world around you—your peers, the media, and so on—that have become your walls, your barriers?

I want to stretch this idea by suggesting that what we think is our direct experience of ourselves may indeed be a confabulation (a partial fabrication). What do I mean by that?

Imagine that you were hypnotized and given a few posthypnotic suggestions. Let's say that one was for *aphasia,* the loss or impairment of the power to use or comprehend words. The hypnotist informed you that when you awoke, you wouldn't remember the number 6. (Hypnotists actually do things of this nature to demonstrate the actuality of hypnosis.) So, you are told that until the hypnotist does something like snap his fingers, you will not know of the number 6. Now, when you're awakened from hypnosis, the posthypnotic suggestion is in place. The hypnotist asks you to count to 10. You do so, skipping the number 6. The hypnotist shows you a bill for dinner for $65.05. You pay $5.05. To you, there is no number 6.

Now, suppose you were born on June 6, 1966. How old are you?

Let's take this a step further. Imagine the posthypnotic suggestion included something like this: "You'll be able to watch television and listen to the radio, but you won't consciously acknowledge the promptings from them that urge you to do something; you'll simply do what they tell you to do. When I ask why, you'll make up a reason for acting that way, but you won't be aware that you're doing so."

You see a TV commercial that tells you to buy ABC Magic Cold Remedy because you'll get a cold soon. You buy the drug. When I ask why, you inform me that it's preventive, just in case. You get sick, of course, and later use the product.

Does any of this sound familiar? Are you aware that research has shown that people do just this sort of thing? In one particular study, participants were shown a picture of a person while simultaneously being subliminally presented with a negative word. When they were asked to rate the person, they not only made a negative evaluation, but they also offered a reason for doing so, even though they were totally unaware of the subliminal stimulus.[2] This kind of research has led many scholars to believe that everyone has a "confabulator" that comes up with things to fill in the gaps in memories and actions, just to make sense of some of their beliefs and the things that they do.

The Automatic Self

There are many areas of our lives in which we fail to be aware of ourselves. Research has shown that projecting subliminal cues that represent the characteristics of a significant other onto a target person leads to the transference of emotions—feelings about the significant other are shifted to the target person. One really interesting study showed that men on a somewhat dangerous bridge, when approached with a questionnaire by an attractive researcher who left them her phone number in case they wanted to know about the study she was conducting, were much more likely to phone and request a date than were men relaxing on a park bench. Apparently, the danger and the level of arousal that resulted from this risk were transferred to the female researcher, causing her to appear more attractive—and all of this was outside conscious awareness. In the words of researcher Jonathan Miller: "Human beings owe a surprisingly large proportion of their cognitive and behavioral capacities to the existence of an 'automatic self' of which they have no conscious knowledge and over which they have little voluntary control."[3]

I am particularly fond of the adage: "To thy own self be true." One reason I like it is the fact that knowing ourselves is a journey—an exploration—and one that demands we risk being wrong about everything we think that we know or believe.

The hypnotic effect, propaganda, media bombardment, and the like all influence us in both predictable and unpredictable ways. Violence actually begets violence. Constant stimuli systematically desensitize our levels of arousal, and the result is that it takes more and more and more sex, violence, and gore to meet our stimulus-response requirement. Becoming "dehypnotized" takes much more effort than the snap of someone's fingers. It's incumbent upon each of us to become aware of all the ways we're managed, manipulated, and even ushered into a sort of hive consciousness, if we truly wish to know who we are and why we're here.

If you recognize the hive consciousness, then what do you do next? What if you see that this is true for you—then what? It's only by recognizing the degree to which your authentic self may be compromised that any genuine self-realization can occur. What if you discover that many of your beliefs are based on false assumptions, sound bites, ideologue agendas, and so forth? What do you do then?

Again, I must emphasize that it's only by realizing the "architecture" behind our hive consciousness that we have any hope of breaking free and actually beginning the very personal journey of self-realization.

chapter 2

Memory: Who Am I?

"Memory is a way of holding on to the things you love, the things you are, the things you never want to lose."

— Kevin Arnold

I interviewed a woman on my radio show not long ago about her memory loss. I was particularly struck by one of her experiences: Imagine waking up one morning and not knowing what happened to the last ten years of your life. Lying there in bed with you is a stranger, and stranger still are your surroundings. You remember the person you love and live with, and the individual beside you is definitely not that person.

Imagine, then, that you rise from the bed and go to the window. Everything is unfamiliar. Indeed, you recognize nothing whatsoever except your face reflected in the glass. You wonder, *Where the hell am I?*

Am I My Memory?

Now imagine that you leave and find a bus, a cab, or some other means of transportation to take you home. Once there, you attempt to enter, but your keys don't work, so you knock. The person who answers is your significant other, but standing nearby is someone else, and you obviously just got both of them out of bed. You discover that in point of fact, ten years ago you were in an accident and everything about you seemed to change. This eventually resulted in a divorce, and you and your mate each remarried some three or four years thereafter. Now you've somehow lost all memories from the accident to the present moment.

Imagine having to suddenly adjust to this new reality. *Am I my memories? Do I lose part of myself if I lose memories? If so, how much can I lose and still be me?* After all, when asked: "Who are you?" don't you normally answer by saying your name and what you do for a living? "I'm Jane Doe (or John Smith), and I'm the Safeway manager at Oasis Park Shopping Center."

How do you tell someone who you are? If you forget everything about yourself, then who are you?

Replicating Consciousness

Let's create yet another scenario. Imagine that the technology to move your consciousness from your body to a computer has been perfected. You can live forever and experience a virtual environment full of every imaginable possibility. Like a character in a science-fiction film or a massive multiplayer online role-playing game (MMORPG), you can have sex with anyone, race fast cars, chase danger on every corner, and even invent different yous so that when you "go out" publicly within the confines of your virtual world, you can look any way you wish. This technology is so complete that a mere thought instantly delivers whatever you desire. Your thinking becomes the destiny you experience. If you imagine beauty, it's there; if you seek adventure, it finds you in an instant. You can't be hurt or injured, but you can enjoy, even feel—albeit through artificial nerves—the universe of your creation.

Now, use a little more imagination and assume that your doctor thought your body was dying, so transferring your consciousness to the computer made sense, but he was mistaken. You have somehow miraculously recovered. You're in your body, and since your actual brain doesn't reside in the computer—only a copy of your consciousness—you're also in the machine. The experiences the you-in-the-body has from this day forward will be different from those of the you-in-the-computer. In time, you may not be the same you—or will you?

The Fork in the Road

What if the you-in-the-body lived another 50 years, married, had children, and converted to a religious faith because of a deeply spiritual experience, inadvertently caused by an electromagnetic impulse that occurred just as your consciousness was transferred? What if, while the you-in-the-body lectured to others about wisdom, virtue, and metaphysics, the you-in-the-computer indulged in every pleasurable act imaginable? Indeed, the you-in-the-computer decided to balance life with a little atheistic existentialism. Virtual-you read the likes of Jean-Paul Sartre and Friedrich Nietzsche over and over until you could recite them from memory. To that, the you-in-the-computer added your own brand of objectivism and integrated it all with works by Ayn Rand. Drawing heavily on all three writers, but in particular on Sartre's classic *Being and Nothingness*, you usually spend part of your day writing philosophical treatises.

Fifty years later, are the two yous the same, or do they just share a common memory from half a century ago? Imagine that the scientific community wants to share the two of you with the public, so you're invited to attend a special gala event celebrating a 50-year reunion between the you-in-the-computer and the you-in-the-body. There you both are. Your messages are quite different: one is of life after death, and the other is of life without death.

Two Views

The you-in-the-computer has quite a following of young people, and they plan to attend this special anniversary en masse. Every day they launch their private terminals to connect to your blog and vicariously experience some of the excitement you regularly indulge in. They recite your philosophy and use your treatises to defend the right of the individual to pursue personal satisfaction above all else, as long as it does no harm or is between consenting adults. High school and college debate teams champion your philosophies across the country. Indeed, the you-in-the-computer is more famous than Friedrich Nietzsche, Ayn Rand, and Jean-Paul Sartre combined. Your student supporters and others—former students who encountered your work as long as 40 years ago—all gather to witness this special day.

Now, the you-in-the-body has many followers as well, individuals who tend to be very conservative, religious, and traditional in their moral views. Additionally, for years there has been a cultural divide. A sort of quasi-cultural war is being waged in the media, on a few college campuses (the holdouts are almost all private schools), and elsewhere in society. Opinions are deeply divided and follow no class lines per se. The argument is all about personal rights and freedoms versus some form of intrinsic and higher motive or virtue.

The personal-rights people are divided, which further complicates the scene. Some among this group are interested in maximizing pleasure for self-interest alone; others are concerned with taking wealth from the rich to support those less capable of living a full, self-indulgent lifestyle. They believe that it's the *fault* of the wealthy that poverty exists, and they strive to even the playing field. They don't believe in rewarding hard work; instead, they believe that everyone works equally hard anyway and should therefore earn the same amount. While their aim is to be charitable to those who are truly down-and-out, their scheme would also cover those who don't want to work at all—or at least as little as possible.

The you-in-the body supports such classic conservative principles as limited government, freedom of religion, the right to life, the right to keep and bear arms, and so forth. Your group believes that taxation beyond the scope needed for limited government is a form of enslavement. As such, you find the ideas of those demanding the redistribution of wealth to be wrong. You believe all life is sacred and strongly oppose abortion as a routine means of birth control.

When it comes to religious ideas, public worship, prayer in schools, the use of the word *God* in the Pledge of Allegiance, Christmas displays on public grounds, and so forth, the cultural divide is even deeper. Only recently you and a large number of your followers filed suit under antidiscrimination statutes in federal court, arguing that religious groups have become minorities and are being discriminated against both in public discourse and in the selective enforcement of local and federal laws.

Obviously, this meeting between the two of you—the you-in-the-body and the you-in-the-computer—will be something more than the planners had in mind. There will be no warm, ingratiating exchanges, no friendly queries such as: "What have you been up to?" You know full well each other's positions and strength in these matters of disagreement. What the two of you *don't* know is that you are—or were—one. The physician who arranged the transfer decided it would be best if you were unaware of each other when the you-in-the-body survived.

The planners behind this reunion are aware of the differences in your lifestyles, but they've underestimated how deep this divide actually is. Further, they've mistakenly imagined each of you warmly welcoming the other—a miscalculation on the scale of that of a former United States President and his staff who imagined a warm welcome in Iraq once Saddam Hussein was overthrown. Insurrection may not be far from what the two of you and your respective groups could create.

Meeting Yourself

The day arrives, and there you are—both of you. You-in-the-body looks upon the image of you-in-the-computer through a giant monitor set up for thousands in the audience to see and hear. You find no likeness to yourself whatsoever. Both of you believe that you have been brought together for a discussion as part of a larger panel. The lead scientist (LS) steps to the podium and announces to the audience and both yous of the real reason for the gathering: this is a reunion of two who once were one. In the interest of science and the public at large, it's time to inform the world about research that has been going on behind the scenes for 50 years.

The two yous look at each other. Total disbelief falls over both of you. LS continues with more details, and suddenly the you-in-the-computer makes the connection and exclaims loudly, "Oh, shit, it *is* you. I can't believe I was ever that innocent or stupid."

The you-in-the-body considers the information being described by LS and challenges the you-in-the-computer: "Tell me something about me that only I could know."

The you-in-the-computer responds with a detail that, although embarrassing, nevertheless meets the criteria perfectly.

The two yous exchange a long stare. The deep animus felt by each of you toward the other suffers a moment of confusion. The conversation then continues between the two of you, ignoring all others. You debate each other's positions with equal fervor and intellect. Pure data and quotation power goes to you-in-the-computer; but pure feeling, the emotional passion that charges the argument, goes to you-in-the-body. It's a dead heat as far as the audience is concerned—this debate between the two of you.

Then the you-in-the-computer turns the debate personal: "Well, if you're wrong and there is no God, you'll die, and I'll continue to live. If I'm right, and there is no God, then look at all the pleasure I've lavished on myself that you've denied in the name of nothing. In fact, when I think about it, I win either way. In either event, I continue, regardless."

There's a pause, and the you-in-the-body answers, "No, not quite. My eschatology [belief regarding end times] will deliver you from the computer one day when all the plugs get pulled. On that day, the last day, the good will be saved and all else will end. You see, only the eternal is real, and therefore only the eternal shall survive. Now with that said, I do see some advantage to your environment versus mine. I can see that you've exerted great influence over the minds of many from your position in the machine. I'll therefore make arrangements for my consciousness, as it is today, to transition to the computer upon the death of my body. From there, I'll have until those last days to answer your slurs and set straight the record regarding the fruits of your selfishness. For it is written: 'You shall know them by their fruits.'"

With that, the you-in-the-body turns and walks away, with your entire following parading behind. In time, the transition is made.

What do you think happens? Which is the real you? What if the new-you-in-the-computer consciousness turned away from what the first two of you believed? Is this just a thought experiment void of any real meaning, or do you find the question regarding the real you worth investigating? How did you become you after all?

chapter 3

True Being

*"We can never judge the lives of others, because each
person knows only their own pain and renunciation. It's
one thing to feel that you are on the right path, but it's
another to think that yours is the only path."*

— ATTRIBUTED TO PAULO COELHO

I watched as passengers disembarked from the plane
I was about to take to Los Angeles, and I saw many
stories in their faces. I thought of the personal tales each
one could tell. I remembered how deceiving looks could
be from my work in criminalistics. Still, my mind was
intent on finding a story for each.

There was a large, older gentleman with huge hands
and veins standing out on his arms like those of a much
younger man who had just finished working out. Next
to him was a small, slightly built man with a cane.
Perhaps the large man had been a bodyguard and the
small one a watchmaker, or perhaps the large man was
a schoolteacher and the small one a convicted killer
released from prison after 40 years behind bars.

What is it that seems to force us to both make up stories about others and to jump to conclusions based upon appearances?

Plato invested much of his life in the quest to understand and make known the true nature of being. His student Aristotle later called this *metaphysics,* the study of being, and *ontology* is its central branch. Is there such a thing as true being? Many since Plato, particularly in the so-called postmodern era, have looked at this notion as problematic at the very least, and at the worst, pure rubbish.

Form and Particular

You may remember Plato's allegory of the cave. In this tale, people who dwelt in the cave could know only the shadows of forms that were cast on the wall of the cave from the light outside. To be clear: from within the cave, inhabitants could only look at shadows on the wall and not the form itself that was casting the shadow.

The shadows were representative of forms—true forms that lacked the distortion of the shapes on the cave wall. With this, the idea of the form and the particular was advanced.

You and I are particulars; your favorite chair is a particular. Think about it this way: There are many kinds of chairs. Some have arms, some have four legs, some swivel, some rock, and so forth. What is it about a chair that makes you immediately apprehend it as a chair, even if you've never seen that particular type before? To Plato, it's the form that we might call "chairness" that makes the object recognizable. Is there such a form for personhood? Is there one form for female and another for male?

"True Being"

Is there such a thing as a "true being" in the onto-logical sense other than what we might appear to be here and now? Is our being dynamic and changing? If so, how do we continue to recognize it as our real, true being?

You might say that chairs are artifacts and humans are biological expressions of living material, so they aren't comparable in the sense of chairness and human-ness. If so, does that alter the question in any substantial way? If not, what is meant by true being?

Knowing or Believing?

Let's once again do some mind traveling and see if we can get close enough to this question to either dis-card it as irrelevant or to know it personally in a way that may illuminate the issue. To that end, imagine you're a student of some great early philosopher. You are witnessing an exchange between a citizen and your teacher.

Citizen asks, "What is being? What does it mean to be human? Is there a true being—a higher being? Are we but meat machines winding down toward an end that destroys all that I think I am and may become?"

Your mentor—I shall call him "Spa," using the first letters in the names *Socrates, Plato,* and *Aristotle*—tells everyone to sit. Spa begins by asking Citizen: "What do you think is likely to happen when your mortal body gives up the ghost?"

You think about that, too. Intuitively, you feel that all of what you've learned, all of who you've become, all that you remember and have shared, couldn't just disappear—be gone, be but a waste of nature's resources. Or could it?

Citizen answers: "How do I know with any certainty what I think about such an issue when it's all wrapped up with my own wants and desires?"

Spa smiles. "What you ask is something that has been asked for a very long time. What we seek to know is bound up in the notion of the form. Is there any such thing as a pure form that's the perfect essence of the particular? Is there a perfect form of *chairness* behind all chairs? Is there a perfect form of humanness behind all humans? Is it possible that it's our belief in a perfect form that we anthropomorphize into our gods? Or is it that we wish so intensely for life to go on that we create a theogony [origin and descent of the gods] in the first place? What are your thoughts, Citizen?"

The expression on Citizen's face indicates that he is no longer present. He is far away in his mind. Finally, the protracted silence that follows Spa's last question suddenly breaks into his consciousness, and he blurts out, "I know what I believe. That's all that matters to me."

Choosing Your Beliefs

Patiently, Spa says ever so softly, "Is what you believe what you want to believe? Are you just so annoyed at lacking an answer that you stake such a bold claim? From whence did your belief come?"

"I know there is a God. I know God through my religion. I've read many books, and I go to church. There's nothing remaining for me to ask," answers Citizen.

"Have you thought about asking—I mean, in your prayers could you ask something like: 'What would you like me to know, God?' Are you open to that?"

Citizen looks quizzically at Spa, afraid of being trapped. Then he says, "I see no harm in asking that."

"Okay. Then may I ask you another question?"

"Go ahead," Citizen replies, feeling more confident.

"What if you ask God just what I suggested, and the answer comes back something along the lines that it would be good for you to use your great mind and senses to explore and know the world and its beliefs before you opt to grab one and stop there? Think for a moment. What if you have it wrong? Do you really want to know, or are you content to think that you know without ever really being sure? Real knowledge is possessing some information, something that you can say with an epistemological certainty: This I know!"

Citizen's head tips slightly as though he is processing something deep within his mind.

Spa continues, "Do you know that one of the rites necessary to enter the Pythagorean brotherhood required that you appear before the entire brotherhood and state what it was that you knew with a certainty. You were first sent out into the desert to think on this, and when you had arrived at what you knew for certain, you returned. The brotherhood was assembled, and once you made your knowledge claim before them, the entire brotherhood would mock, ridicule, question, and otherwise attempt to dissuade you. If you were unable to make an adequate defense or weren't truly convinced of your claim, it soon became obvious. Only those who could withstand this assault without disavowing their knowledge were admitted. Is your knowledge of that certain kind?"

Citizen shrugs his shoulders, gets up, and walks away.

What Do You Know?

What is it that you know with certainty? You know it through and through. It's as real to you as your being—but not the being René Descartes doubted when he thought of himself as perhaps an item in someone's dream.[1] No, if we admit that notion, then is there anything we can say we know for certain?

Descartes began his musings by doubting his very existence. Suddenly an epiphany: "Cogito ergo sum," or "I think, therefore I am." I'll restate that in context: "I doubt, therefore I am."

What am I? For Descartes, I am a thinking, doubting agency; and obviously, therefore, I am a mind. This thinking spawned what we know today as mind-body dualism.

"I doubt, therefore I am" may have made perfect sense to Descartes, but this kind of doubt is forever destined to doubt. Perhaps the dreamer who imagined you wishes you to doubt your being, so doubt itself is only a circular motion in thought and not an answer. Indeed, many great philosophers have contended with Descartes' doubt, which led to the duality of mind and body, and on more than one occasion it has been essentially set aside as ridiculous.[2] No, what we seek is a level of knowing that we could classify as beyond a reasonable doubt.

Is your knowledge that certain, and if so, how? If not, why not? What if everything you believe is wrong? Can you even admit that possibility?

chapter 4

The Lucifer Effect

"Evil (ignorance) is like a shadow—it has no real substance of its own; it is simply a lack of light. You cannot cause a shadow to disappear by trying to fight it, by stamping on it, by railing against it, or by any other form of emotional or physical resistance. In order to cause a shadow to disappear, you must shine light on it."

— SHAKTI GAWAIN

A young woman leaves the high school homecoming dance and phones her father to come pick her up. She then walks toward the parking lot and begins her wait. At some point she finds herself the victim of a gang rape. CNN Justice reported this story opening this way:

> For more than two hours on a dark Saturday night, as many as 20 people watched or took part as a 15-year-old California girl was allegedly gang raped and beaten outside a high school homecoming dance, authorities said.
>
> As hundreds of students gathered in the school gym, outside in a dimly lit alley where the victim was allegedly raped, police say witnesses took photos. Others laughed.

"As people announced over time that this was going on, more people came to see, and some actually participated," Lt. Mark Gagan of the Richmond Police Department told CNN.

The witnesses failed to report the crime to law enforcement, Gagan said. The victim remained hospitalized in stable condition. Police arrested five suspects and more arrests were expected.

So why didn't anyone come forward?[1]

The Genovese Effect

Such a scenario is often referred to as the bystander, or Genovese, effect, after Catherine "Kitty" Genovese, who was attacked over a 30-minute period. Despite the large number of people who heard her screams for help, no one did anything to come to her aid. The first phone call to law enforcement wasn't made until a full half hour after the attack began. Unfortunately, Kitty Genovese was stabbed to death before police arrived.[2] As with the rape victim at her homecoming dance, by the time law enforcement reached the scene, it was simply too late—the crime had already been committed. What makes a reasonably good human being capable of ignoring events of this nature? How can one just ignore such brutality? It's generally thought that it's easier to turn away when there are multiple parties witnessing something, for after all, someone else will tend to it. This is the effect of a crowd.

The Vulture and the Child

There's a classic photograph that won a Pulitzer Prize and perhaps led the photographer to take his own life. The photo, taken by Kevin Carter in 1993, is of a Sudanese child being followed by a vulture. Carter, a South African photojournalist, stated that he watched the child apparently trying to crawl for help or food for some 20 minutes while waiting for the vulture to spread its wings because he thought this would make a better picture. This photo of a Sudanese child at the brink of starvation, obviously seriously emaciated, won Carter the Pulitzer for photojournalism. Carter took the shot, frightened the bird away, and then left. He later stated that he didn't want to get involved. Some say the parents had gone ahead to an aid station for food and the child was attempting to reach them, but what happened to the child is anyone's guess. We do know that Carter took his own life a year after receiving the Pulitzer.[3] Guilt? Remorse? What do you think you would do?

As I continue to examine these issues, I remind you that you may find some of these thought experiments and examples upsetting—or at the least, controversial.

The Lucifer Effect

In his book *The Lucifer Effect,* Philip Zimbardo showcases the worst of humankind. With the skills one could expect from a past president of the American Psychological Association, Zimbardo reveals the hard research that illustrates clearly the evil that rests within all of us, awaiting only the right circumstances before it's released. From his landmark Stanford prison experiment to his assessment and evaluation of the facts behind the abuse of prisoners at Abu Ghraib, collecting and reporting on multifarious relevant research along the way, Zimbardo makes it absolutely clear that the majority of people will deny ever being able to ignore the commission of an evil act, let alone actually being able do something evil. Yet the statistical probability is that these denials are only that—they don't address reality. In other words, it may make you feel good to deny this propensity, but the denial doesn't make it a fact. In the real world, it would appear that awareness, alertness to the possibility and the causes that underlie this potential, are the only true defense against falling prey to what Zimbardo aptly tagged "the Lucifer Effect."[4]

So is it fair to ask about such things as virtue if this tendency is built into the system of being human? Few of us, if we're genuinely honest with ourselves, can state that we've never had a thought containing a seed of violence. Many of us enjoy entertainment that offers the vicarious ability to exact judgment or revenge for imagined or pretended deeds. We watch movies that provoke this instinct. Moviemakers know how to make the villain truly nefarious and thereby incite our passions. We side with the "good guy" and cheer as he or she justifiably does the villain in. Indeed, blockbuster movies are almost always thrillers and the good-guy/bad-guy epic is as old as literature itself, for this is just the portrayal of the struggle between good and evil.

Real Virtue

What is good? Is there any real virtue? Plato struggled with this idea thousands of years ago. He insisted in his work *The Republic* that there was a pure form of virtue. That is, there are many virtues, such as honesty, kindness and so forth, but only one true essence of virtue.

As discussed earlier in this book, in his allegory of the cave, Plato developed the idea of a form that transcended the particular. Using his metaphor, imagine that you're a cave dweller. In fact, you're chained to a wall in the cave in such a way that you can't turn your head. You look straight ahead. There's a fire in the cave, and its glow casts shadows on the wall in front of you, but you can't see what makes the shadows.

For Plato, this is the world we dwell in. Recall that the shadow is a particular, say a particular chair, but not the form *chairness*. In order to gain access to the form, one must turn away from the shadow and come out of the cave into the true light of day—forget about the fire. Plato believed that doing this required discipline, which he called *dialectic*. Question and question and question again until a point of clarity can be reached—this was the Socratic method, or way to truth. For Plato, there was an absolute virtue.[5] For many philosophers and thinkers since, however, not only does Plato's method fail to satisfactorily produce an essence or ultimate form, but they also believe it's problematic to assume that there's any such thing.

I recently had a conversation with a popular New Age leader on my weekly radio show—Neale Donald Walsch, the author of *Conversations with God* and other best-selling books. Neale essentially stated that there were no universal virtues. Indeed, he asserted that values were relative—an argument for cultural relativity (the idea that good and bad are relative to culture).[6]

I had a problem with that statement. For me, the evolution of consciousness—single cell to man, monkey to man, Cro-Magnon to Homo sapiens, or whatever—does not exist without the recognition of our sense of service to one another; our intuitive knowledge that some things are just inherently wrong; our realization that there are causes, purposes, meanings, and so forth that are larger than the individual.

Value Systems

The study of values is called *axiology*. Metaphysics is all about ontology (being) and axiology (values). Philosophers have long labored over values, absolute to relative. Immanuel Kant, the 18th-century German philosopher, reasoned that value systems couldn't necessarily be relied upon due to tradition, religion, and the like, for in his view there was nothing unconditionally good except goodwill. He therefore insisted that goodwill was the basic premise from which values derive their authority.[7]

My question to Neale began with acts of violent cruelty such as those by a father who runs down his daughter because she is becoming too "westernized." His reply suggested that this was okay, for what else could you expect from someone who'd been raised to believe it was okay? Well, for me and Kant and a whole host of others, there's nothing kindly, nothing remotely similar to "goodwill," in an act of this nature. It's purely selfish, lower-animal behavior, like that of a stallion that kills a foal so that he can get to a mare. Where is the enlightened consciousness in this?

Common Values

Following the interview with Neale, I enjoyed a conversation with two men I admire: neurosurgeon John L. Turner and NASA physicist Tom Campbell, who joined me for an hour on the phone. Our conversation was all about consciousness. We agreed that everything (all that is) is consciousness dealing with a data stream, as in a multiplayer virtual game. Our understanding of the laws of physics constitutes the rules for the game. We make changes in our individual realities by the way we interpret this data stream and as a result of our interactions with others. In this model, our relationships and our mutual interpretations reinforce the world as we know it.

Leaving the theory there for just a minute, what should we do when two opposing views arise? Simple— we discuss those views in an adult manner, hoping to gain from the exchange and not subtract from the other.

Therefore, Neale and I disagreed and had a relatively civil discussion about our opposition. I asserted that the world would never know peace if we couldn't come to some point where there was common virtue—common values that we could then uphold with the rule of law. In my opinion, that might begin by deciding that life was sacred. In this great country, we view it all through the eyes of our founding fathers: that we were created with certain inalienable rights—life, liberty and the pursuit of happiness.

Neale's answer was along the lines that people should do exactly whatever 50 percent plus one agree upon.

We live in a so-called modern era where tradition is often discarded. In this culturally relevant modernism, there exists little coherence in values or ethics. There are those who say something similar to what Neale suggested when he said, "Eldon, you expect people to be consistent, and they're not."

He's right. I want coherence, consonance—not dissonance—and I do believe that enlightenment demands this. The philosopher Alasdair Chalmers MacIntyre believes that a historical narration of the development of ethics is necessary in order to illuminate the modern problem of moral arguments that proceed from incompatible premises. In his seminal work *After Virtue,* he identifies the central question of morality as having to do with the habits and knowledge concerning how to live a good life. His approach seeks to demonstrate that good judgment emanates from good character.[8]

Agendas

What, then, is good character? Does it mean holding on to morally relevant beliefs? Is there any dissonance in what you believe?

Sometimes moral lines are grayed deliberately. Those with agendas have a way of reframing definitions, and little by little eroding principles. Let's take this example: You probably find it repugnant when someone stabs a pregnant woman, killing her and her unborn child. In some states, such as California, the perpetrator would be prosecuted for a double murder. In that same state, however, abortions are common, and sometimes that includes late-term abortions. The law regarding criminal homicide doesn't distinguish with respect to just "how pregnant" the victim must be. Indeed, if she's only three weeks pregnant, it's still a double homicide.

How can we have two such laws, one that argues for the sanctity of life, including the life of an unborn child, and one that so totally disregards the same? The answer is simple: disguise the issue. Make it an issue of rights or choice, the right of a mother to her body or her right to choose, and there's no longer a right to life.

Dissonance is often inherent in our modern interpretations and definitions. Recently an employee of Planned Parenthood publicly announced that the organization encourages abortions because it makes more money by performing them. In her words: "Every meeting that we had was, 'We don't have enough money. We don't have enough money—we've got to keep these abortions coming.' It's a very lucrative business, and that's why they want to increase numbers."[9] She was unsuccessfully sued by Planned Parenthood.

Abby Johnson worked and volunteered with Planned Parenthood for eight years. "She recently quit after watching the ultrasound of an abortion. She claimed watching the baby 'crumple' as it was vacuumed from a woman's uterus changed her heart and opinion towards abortion."[10] Indeed, in a Fox television interview, she remarked further about just how hard the baby appeared to be struggling to escape and live.

One personal friend of mine went to the Internet and searched images involving abortion. She came away shocked, and her opinion had changed. Where before she had completely defended the practice, she now was totally opposed. She admitted to being *dumbed down* and remembered how the original time period for legal abortions had been stretched out again and again. While she had experienced great joy when reading the week-by-week account of her own baby's development in the womb, she had simply disconnected this information from the rights of the mother. She'd stopped thinking about how well developed her own baby had been at only a few weeks. Instead, the argument had become one of 12 versus 40 weeks. It took 40 weeks for the baby to reach maturity/independence, so at 12 weeks it couldn't be sufficiently developed for it to take precedence over the mother's desires.

Perhaps my friend's thinking process was a little like being desensitized to an issue by definitions, and as a result she found herself going along with the crowd. Remember the effect of the crowd from earlier—do nothing, say nothing, just as with the Genovese effect. Why? Because everyone else thinks it's okay or even right. Those who don't agree have been defined in unflattering ways, and no one wishes to be described like that. What is the percentage in getting involved? What if people on all sides of such issues took the time to examine their thought processes? What if you did the same?

First Principles

By now it's easy to see that my notion of a first principle that everyone could agree upon—say, the right to life—isn't so easy to come by. How on earth will the world ever know peace if something as fundamental as the right to life can't be defined and agreed upon? In some cultures, if you treat your father in an undignified manner, casting shame on the family, it's appropriate that you die. But, as mentioned, in California, killing a pregnant woman is considered to be a double homicide, yet a late-term abortion is considered to be a woman's right. Indeed, according to the California Health Code 123468, abortion is a woman's right, and further, the state may not deny or interfere with her right provided the fetus is not independently viable. With regard to the viable, the code reads: "There is reasonable likelihood of the fetus' sustained survival outside the uterus *without* the application of extraordinary medical measures." What constitutes extraordinary is not clear.[11]

How do you define life? How do you define virtue? Is there such a thing as an essence of good? What is it? Have you thought all of this through before? What if your ideas were wrong—where would you be then? What if you were to discover that your values were all built on dissonant foundations—what then? And what if your values were to dramatically change? Would you still be the same person?

❖❖❖

chapter 5

Blame Is Socially Contagious

"A man can fail many times, but he isn't a failure until he begins to blame somebody else."

— JOHN BURROUGHS

Let's take a real case that occurred in Virginia in 2009 and flavor it with some imagination. Prepare yourself for another intense thought experiment, one designed to evoke strong emotions and push you to examine your thoughts and values.

Pretend you're a character in a movie—indeed, you're the hero or heroine. You're an investigator working for law enforcement, and you're summoned to the scene of a family dispute. Neighbors have called to report yelling and screaming coming from a small apartment in the suburbs of your city. You're greeted at the door by a grandmother in tears, who points to a baby lying on an ottoman not ten feet from the door. You don't immediately realize that the newborn is dead, for it has been only a few minutes.

You look at the baby and panic. Its head is covered with a plastic grocery bag, which is translucent enough that you can see many of the infant's features. The hair is wet and appears dark, high cheekbones rise above lovely lips, a strong nose. The child reminds you of another baby—one you love, perhaps one who has grown up—but for now you frantically work to get the bag off the child's head. Once it's removed, you realize that the baby is dead. Horror and anger rise within you.

The mother is sitting in a chair nearby. She is undisturbed by the whole matter.

You ask, "What happened?"

The story slowly unfolds. The grandmother, through heavy tears, sobs the answer. Her daughter, the child's mother, suffocated the child with a grocery bag. All of this was done quite calmly while the umbilical cord was still attached.

Let's assume that the cord is now cut. The mother rests in the chair within reach of the ottoman. Slowly, she puts her feet up, crossing them right next to the dead child. You're aware of the law, so you know there's nothing illegal about what just happened. That means there's nothing you can do. You can call in the coroner, but the law is technically on the mother's side, for it states that as long as the umbilical cord is attached, the child isn't independently viable. While this law was originally designed to protect those assisting in a delivery that resulted in a stillbirth, this loophole is obviously a terrible problem. What do you do?

Some might be tempted to enforce their own justice to some measure. Perhaps you make the arrest on the grounds that the umbilical cord was cut before the child died. Perhaps you even go so far as to falsify some of the evidence—after all, the grandmother is so distraught that she isn't really clear about the order of events. You persuade her that her daughter must have cut the cord before the child actually died. That means the bag could and should have been removed, because the child at that point was a viable life entity and no longer dependent upon the mother for survival. What else could you do? Could you just walk away and say, "Oh, well"?

Let's assume you're a straight arrow and wouldn't falsify a police report just to punish this mother. You ask her what happened. She quite plainly states that she didn't want the baby, so she smothered it with the bag before cutting the cord. Not only is she not remorseful, but she's actually glad she did it. You call the police station, the coroner comes and removes the body, and you head to the station to write up the report. Once you've completed that perfunctory detail, you go home. How do you feel?

Another Day

The next day, you tell your friends about the previous night and the drama with the newborn child. You all protest the wrongfulness of the law, then go for coffee and doughnuts. It's a new day—just another day, and life goes on. But does it?

At what point do you become an activist? When do you decide to take the matter into your own hands and change the law? When do you conclude that something isn't okay just because the crowd signals it's okay—or in this instance, legal?

What an awful mother to do such a thing. She should at least be forced to undergo psychiatric evaluation. Sick woman! These are your thoughts as you set about your rounds. Today you have a handful of bench warrants. As you look them over, you see that they're all the result of people's failure to appear (FTA) in court. Looking closer, you also note that in every instance, the FTA involves a traffic infraction. "There are real criminals to catch, and I'm turned into a process server," you grumble.

Your first stop is a rundown trailer in a trailer park right out of an old horror movie. You knock on the door and a man answers. You show your badge and inform him of the warrant: he can either pay the $199 fine, or you'll take him to jail. He explains that he doesn't have a job. He was laid off six months ago when the business he worked for closed its doors and filed for bankruptcy. He didn't go to court because he knew he'd have a traffic fine, and he couldn't pay it. He says that he thought they'd mail him something like a bill, and he'd have some time to pay it. He pleads with you not to take him to jail.

He's a single father, and his four sons, ages 4 through 11, stand behind him at the door. You ask about their mother and learn she was killed in an auto accident three years ago. It seems that a car thief escaped from jail and stole another car. A high-speed chase ensued, and as the mother was going through an intersection on a green light, the thief broadsided her car. Police had turned their sirens off because they were approaching a school zone, and they didn't want to force the criminal into that area. The young mom's vehicle was T-boned without warning, and she was killed on the spot.

Justice Is Served?

The law says you must bring this man in. Do you? Where's the justice if you let the woman who killed her own child remain free while you arrest this single parent and place his four children with child protective services over a traffic fine?

These are real events that real people face and deal with. Where's the equity? What if you had the power to do something about this? Would you?

In the last chapter, we discussed the pressure that peers or a crowd can put on a person. It should be noted that the more ability individuals have to remain anonymous, the less likely they are to come to the aid of another. What is it about the human condition that leads us to sleep through injustices and leave their correction to someone else?

Taking Action

As for the *What if?* situation above, you *do* have the power to do something about it. Imagine if everyone in this country simply wrote a quick letter to their local government—whatever branch had the power to make the change—whenever something of this kind was brought to their attention. What would be the result?

There's a great deal of charity in America. This country is open to sharing and giving to those in need. Is it just as concerned about these injustices? Or is the difference one of definition? That is, we all recognize the poor and undernourished child, the starved and beaten animal, so it's easy to give to charities that help them. However, it's not as easy to get involved in changing a system we disagree with. For one thing, we don't all agree on what's an injustice; and even if we did, it's generally easier to remain anonymous and leave these decisions up to someone else to correct. It's easier to give a dollar than to give of our time. What other excuses can you think of?

Not long ago, one of my readers sent me this:

> For too long we have been too complacent about the workings of Congress. Many citizens had no idea that members of Congress could retire with the same pay after only one term, that they specifically exempted themselves from many of the laws they have passed (such as being exempt from any fear of prosecution for sexual harassment) while ordinary citizens must live under those laws. The latest was to exempt themselves from the health-care reform—in all of its forms. Somehow, that doesn't seem logical. We do not have an elite that is above the law. I truly don't care if they are Democrat, Republican, Independent or whatever. The self-serving must stop.
>
> A Constitutional convention—this is a good way to do that. I'm asking each addressee to forward this e-mail to a minimum of 20 people on their address list; in turn, ask each of those to do likewise. In three days, most people in the United States of America will have the message. This idea's time has come!

Proposed 28th Amendment to the United States Constitution

"Congress shall make no law that applies to the citizens of the United States that does not apply equally to the Senators and/or Representatives; and, Congress shall make no law that applies to the Senators and/or

Representatives that does not apply equally to the citizens of the United States."

What would you do if you received something like this—send it on or ignore it? Would you satisfy your conscience by sending it on so that you could forget about it—the Pontius Pilate method? Would you look up its claims regarding current laws to see if they were actually true? Are members of Congress really exempt in these ways? What if everyone who received this actually made it a priority issue—what would happen then?

When all is said and done and you look back on your life, will you be happy with both your actions and your inactions? If this existence is a parade that passes by only once, then you should maximize your pleasure and minimize your pain. Yet somehow I don't think you believe that, or you wouldn't be reading this book.

Then what *does* matter? It's easy to be anonymous, turn over decisions, give up responsibility, and thereby become inauthentic. What if you decided to be authentic at every level of your being today—what would that mean? What would you have to change? How would you even go about finding your authentic self? Or do you already know all there is to know about "you"? If you don't, whose fault is it?

It would be easy to judge the mother who suffocated her child and blame her for the evil act, but only if you thought it was wrong. Systematically, our society has desensitized our value system over the past 50 years or so to such an extent that it's sometimes hard to believe that America is the same country it was just after World War II. What we see on prime-time television would have shocked the generation that fought that war. The first-person shooter games that we raise our children on are nothing more than killing simulators. Some learn to fly an airplane in a simulator, but many more are learning to kill, and they're being systematically desensitized to the horror of it in the process. It's not uncommon to hear young people cheer in a movie when someone is about to be murdered or raped. Many will laugh and shout such things as: "Get her!" Who's to blame for this?

Video Games

Research shows the effect that video games, including massive multiplayer online role-playing games (MMORPGs), have on their players. But before I take that on, allow me to give you a short history of video games and violent media to show how in just a short time, the most innocent of media can become legal trainers and desensitizing machines for killers.

In 1972, the first video entertainment game stormed onto the scene. Most of us who are old enough to remember it played it—*Pong.* Two players used video paddles to hit a ball back and forth, much as a Ping-Pong game would be played. In the late 1980s and early '90s, one-on-one fighting games arrived on the scene. Among them was *Mortal Kombat,* which raised the violence bar. In 1992, *Wolfenstein* was the first major 3-D first-person-shooter game; it placed the player right in the game, fighting, killing, and being killed. The realism in *Wolfenstein* rose to a new level as well, with enemies falling and bleeding on the floor. It provoked a revolution in games.

In 1993, *Doom* arrived, involving much blood and gore and allowing players to hunt and kill each other. As the technical and graphic capability increased, the games became more and more explicit and real. Today, games of this nature, such as *Soldier of Fortune* "respond realistically to different shots depending on where in the body they are shot, with what weapons and from what distance."[1]

Most have the wrong idea of who plays video games, for the average gamer isn't a teenager. No, it's actually an overweight 35-year-old man who's aggressive, introverted, and often depressed, according to the Centers for Disease Control. Some believe that war games honor our veterans, yet the veterans themselves say the opposite. In a recent conversation, radio host Jason Spiess pointed out that when he asked veterans on Veterans Day: "How do we honor you?" the nearly unanimous answer was: "Find ways to resolve conflict peacefully." Veterans went on to point out that war games dishonor their service because the games not only glamorize it, but also distort the reality of it. Indeed, a proposed new game called *Six Days in Fallujah* has met with public opposition by veterans' groups for precisely these reasons.

Here are some facts I want you to consider. First-person-shooter games have been linked to an increase in hostile aggressive behavior and a reduction in pro-social behaviors such as charitable giving, volunteer work, and overall helping behaviors. According to one report: "Video games account for one-third of the average monthly core entertainment spending in the U.S. and . . . nearly a third of the avid gamers are in the 6- to 17-year-old age group."[2]

When men were assigned to play *Grand Theft Auto,* their blood pressure increased, they reported more permissive attitudes toward drugs and alcohol, and they exhibited uncooperative behavior.[3] Adolescents who play more than one hour a day manifest more intense symptoms of ADHD, and game usage has been linked to lower scores on SAT tests and lower grade point averages. One study found that "those who play MMORPGs report more hours spent playing, worse health, worse sleep quality, and greater interference in 'real-life' socializing and academic work versus those playing other types of video games."[4]

Positron-emission tomography (PET) scans taken when young men played a video game in which they moved a tank around a battlefield to destroy the enemy showed that the neurotransmitter dopamine—involved with feelings of reward—was released in the brain. The researcher stated, "This and other studies suggest that the release of dopamine and stress hormones may be related not only to ideas of violence and harm, but also to motivation."[5] This refers to motivation to play more video games, which offers a possible explanation for why the hobby is so addictive.

Still other studies employing functional magnetic resonance imaging (fMRI) have shown exactly what areas of the brain are involved when playing violent video games. Researchers have found that:

> ". . . immediately before firing a weapon, players displayed greater activity in the dorsal anterior cingulate cortex. This area controls cognitive control and planning, among other functions. While firing a weapon and shortly afterward, players showed less activity in the rostral anterior cingulate cortex and amygdala. Because

interaction between these brain areas is associated with resolving emotional conflict, their decreased functioning could indicate a suppression of the emotional response to witnessing the results of taking violent action." [6]

Who's to Blame?

This leads to a systematic desensitization, which in turn leads to a general numbing of empathy—to say nothing of the direct correlation with the increase in hostile aggressive behavior. Add to this common television programs and other entertainment, and an average young adult will have seen more than 200,000 commercials and more than 30,000 homicides.[7]

The fact is that more than 1,000 studies, including reports from the National Institutes of Health and the U.S. Surgeon General's office, suggest overwhelmingly that there's a definite causal connection between media violence and aggressive behavior in some individuals. I think of it this way: Take young people and put them in simulators designed to teach them to kill without emotion. Show them all the blood and gore, and reward them for a successful kill. Add greater and greater rewards to enhance their abilities. Soon, you have trained killers who are free from guilt, remorse, or a nagging conscience. We train pilots in flight simulators; some of our enemies do the same thing and carry out their missions as a result. What on earth do we think we're doing to the younger generation? Once again I ask: "Who's to blame?"

Many people will answer that question with a firm "Not me!" It's the profit motive; it's the game companies;

it's Congress that should pass stricter laws; it's parents who let their children have these games; it's the retailer who sells them . . . and on and on.

While we're assigning blame, let's understand that according to a recent study, blaming is socially contagious: "Nathanael J. Fast, assistant professor of management at the University of Southern California (USC), and Larissa Tiedens, professor of organizational behavior at Stanford, found that publicly blaming others dramatically increases the likelihood that the practice will become viral [likely to spread]."[8] Do we have a new viral means to escape personal responsibility, and is it called blame?

Forgiveness

It's popular today to practice forgiveness. The benefits have been shown to improve everything from success with money to health and overall happiness.[9] So in their personal lives, many people at least try to forgive. One of the profound benefits is that this undoes your ability to blame and therefore directly empowers you. For as long as you hold someone else responsible, to the precise extent that you blame someone or something else, you rob yourself of the power to act. In other words, if you blame your parents for the way you are, then it's not your fault and there's not much you can do about it now. It's akin to crying over spilled milk. You think, *Ah, but for the grace of God, everyone would be exactly where I am because it's not my fault—it was done to me.*

Let's assume it really was done to you—whatever the "it" was. What are you going to do about that? Blaming is not fixing; blaming is giving up. It's easy to point at someone else and seek acceptance, or at least it's much easier than taking responsibility and doing something proactive about it. So, your parents verbally abused you and made you feel insecure. How about forgiving them and getting on with becoming secure? Why should you forgive them? It's simple: until you do, you can't really move on. You remain tied to those feelings of blame, which usually include anger, fear, shame, and more. Perhaps you'd like to be whole, so you forgive and take responsibility for turning a negative into a positive.

Does this same principle of self-responsibility apply to our social order? Should we all be activists of some sort? Is it our obligation to speak up when we think things have gone wrong? Is living in a democracy an opportunity, an obligation, or both? What if it were your daughter who did the suffocating in the story at the beginning of this chapter? Would you feel any more inclined to become active with respect to what's moral and what isn't? Or would you acquiesce into complacency and blame it on the system, the politicians, the greedy corporations, and the like?

Unfortunately, that's exactly what most people do in our Western civilized world, and I do say *civilized* facetiously. For how can we be truly advanced and allow these things to go on without at least speaking out? I could be wrong . . . but what if I'm not?

chapter 6

The Spiritual Quest

*"The great awareness comes slowly, piece by piece. The path
of spiritual growth is a path of lifelong learning."*

— M. Scott Peck

Blame builds a culture of fear and leads to disempowering our inherent right to maximize our experience in life. This maximization of ourselves is what psychologist Abraham Maslow termed our *hierarchy of needs*.[1] At the top is our spiritual growth, and nowhere is our need for personal responsibility more appropriate than with matters of spirituality. That said, how many of us have simply taken the word of another for what we believe?

On Retreat

What if you found yourself at a retreat, similar to the one in Arizona in 2009? The leader is excited as he invites everyone to experience the real, unlimited self. The tempo of his voice increases as the pitch and cadence of his delivery rises and falls like a musical masterpiece. The excitement is contagious, and soon everyone is feeling the excitement—some even have goose bumps. All of this is leading to a special exercise that will cleanse you forever of your doubts and fears. It's as if you're about to be asked to walk on hot coals—but that's not the deal today. No, today it's not a fire walk, not rappelling down some steep building or cliff, not a bungee jump or anything like that—no, today's event sounds much safer, so you've ventured here to participate in the Native American sweat-lodge tradition.

When the group is prepared, the leader shows you into the lodge, which is a large tent. The air is very hot and thick. Some chanting begins, and the leader speaks more softly now, as though he's about to guide everyone through a dream. As time passes, the air grows ever heavier, and you have more and more trouble breathing. You're all told not to leave the tent. "Don't quit when you're almost there. Don't quit just before the miracle," the leader urges.

The person next to you is gasping—you can tell she's about to collapse. A woman across from you falls backward from her sitting position as though she has just passed out. You can't believe how difficult it is to breathe. The sweat pours off you. You're oscillating between some form of full ordinary consciousness and some sort of out-there trip. You question yourself: *Am I supposed to feel this way? Are they burning some kind of hallucinogenic?*

You're about to speak out when another woman attempts to stand, only to fall on her face. You think, *Two down and a third—maybe a fourth, counting me—are about to fall.* It dawns on you in a sudden epiphany: *I could die in here, and no one would know until much later.* Then you wonder, *Are those two women okay?*

At what point do you take the initiative to check on yourself and others? At what juncture do you realize that your leader may just be a little unreliable for this kind of thing? Let's assume that you're lucid enough to recall how you got there. You didn't fill out a health record or any other form that might disclose either physical or mental conditions. No one asked you about your fitness for this sort of thing. Some of those in the lodge are clearly in better shape than others; and some are closer to the tent entrance, thus both farther from the fire and able to breathe more easily.

Seeking Spiritual Insight

You're here to gain spiritual insight. Are you responsible for what's going on around you? Are you responsible for those who are going through this with you? Or have you abrogated your responsibility by turning everything over to the leader?

If you have a genuine insight, you'll claim it as your own. Are you willing to claim the process as yours regardless of what you get out of it? Should you be? Is there any such thing as a genuine spiritual gain that's yours without any personal responsibility? What if your vision leads you to believe that God has instructed you to kill your sister-in-law because she's corrupting your brother? Do you just blindly follow what you think you've been told, or do you take responsibility for your actions? In my book *What Does That Mean?* I tell the story of two brothers who were instructed by God, at least in their minds, to do just this sort of thing and therefore murdered two members of their family.

When do you question even your most deeply held belief? When do you insist that there's no authority high enough to get you to do certain things or, perhaps, ignore certain things?

The Sweat Lodge

So here you are in the sweat lodge. What do you do? Do you just go with it and leave it all to the professionals—the leader and his team *are* professionals, aren't they? Oh, wait. You realize something else: there are no paramedics, nurses, doctors, or other medical professionals on hand. Hold on a minute—did the Native Americans take their doctors to the sweat lodge? Of course not, and these ceremonies have been around forever. What could go wrong?

In October 2009, the *New York Times* reported:

> Midway through a two-hour sweat lodge ceremony intended to be a rebirthing experience, participants say, some people began to fall desperately ill from the heat, even as their leader, James Arthur Ray, a nationally known New Age guru, urged them to press on. . .
>
> "There were people throwing up everywhere," said Dr. Beverley Bunn, 43, an orthodontist from Texas, who said she struggled to remain conscious in the sweat lodge, a makeshift structure covered with blankets and plastic and heated with fiery rocks.
>
> Dr. Bunn said Mr. Ray told the more than 50 people jammed into the small structure—people who had

just completed a 36-hour "vision quest" in which they fasted alone in the desert—that vomiting "was good for you, that you are purging what your body doesn't want, what it doesn't need." But by the end of the ordeal on Oct. 8, emergency crews had taken 21 people to hospitals. Three have since died.

Mr. Ray, who calls himself a teacher of "practical mysticism" and has gained widespread exposure through writings and an appearance on "The Oprah Winfrey Show," has come under intense scrutiny in the New Age movement that is a cottage industry here. The Yavapai County sheriff, Steve Waugh, has opened a homicide investigation, but Mr. Ray has not been charged.

Dr. Bunn, who had signed up for the $9,695 "spiritual warrior" experience, offered the first eyewitness account of the sweat lodge. Details were confirmed by relatives and lawyers for other participants. Dr. Bunn, who has not retained a lawyer and has not decided whether to sue, recounted that Mr. Ray told the group that he had extensive experience in sweat lodges—he holds the "spiritual warrior" event annually—and that his sweats were very intense.

Mr. Ray sat by the tent-flap door, Dr. Bunn said, which remained sealed except for pauses when fresh air briefly circulated as additional rocks heated in an outdoor fire were brought in.[2]

The UK's *Guardian* reported on the event with this headline: "Death Valley: Three New-Agers Die in a Sweat Lodge."[3]

Reporting on upcoming lawsuits over the matter, the online blog *LegalFish: The Daily Tackle*, had this to say:

Three people died and about 20 were hospitalized after two hours in a makeshift sweat lodge, an idea Ray borrowed from Native American tradition. Just like a modern day sauna, the sweat ritual is used for physical and spiritual cleansing. While traditional ceremonies err on the side of caution, limiting their gatherings to 4–12 people and encouraging participants to leave if they feel uncomfortable, Ray urged a crowd of 64—many of whom were falling ill and collapsing on the scene—to stay in the dome-structure that reached temperatures of over 110 degrees.[4]

The Cult Education Forum published these remarks by contributor "Anticult," whose remarks made before the incident seem to forewarn of reasons to think carefully before trusting James Arthur Ray:

Oprah Winfrey is THE person who literally made James Arthur Ray. Oprah put the blatant scam-artist James Ray on her TV show several times, when she did her shows on *The Secret*. Oprah introduced him to her naive audience, and James Ray went to town with it. Before Oprah, James Ray was a nobody. After Oprah, he was able to bilk thousands of people. Oprah did not ask James Arthur Ray ONE single critical question. She didn't check out his background. James Ray was never challenged on a single point or claim he was making. At the EXACT MOMENT he was on her show, there were many very serious complaints about James Ray on Oprah's own message boards.[5]

Responsibility

Anyone can write anything on the Internet, so just how true this statement is should be questioned, of course. As for blame, almost everyone seems able to find someone to pin things on and to have a good deal of desire to do so. Some of the stories and shouts of blame may well be entirely unfounded. Just because someone claims something happened in a particular way doesn't necessarily mean it did. That said, no one is saying anything about the elephant in the room: At what point is the individual responsible for remaining in this environment?

As it turns out, there was at least one medical professional present, albeit as an attendee. Does this participant share any responsibility for ignoring what eventually led to the death of three people?

Research has repeatedly demonstrated that the area of the brain responsible for decision making shuts down when an authority is present. Did the leader actually have that much power, or was it just surrendered to him?

Should there have been intake forms that included a psychological history as well as the usual medical-conditions questionnaire? I think that's a given. Why were none used? To a health-care professional, that in itself should have been a red flag. How many of those in the tent were on medication and what kind? Why were participants in a three-day fast followed by a sweat lodge not prescreened for health issues? Is everyone abdicating responsibility in accordance with the social blame game you've learned about in this chapter?

Bad things do sometimes happen to very good people. Why? No one really can say with absolute certainty, but this much is certainly true: good people seeking a good outcome trusted someone else with their lives, and bad things happened. Leaders and teachers make mistakes, and we're all supposed to know that.

Lawsuits

The *Phoenix New Times* reported on the lawsuits:

A survivor of the "Spiritual Warrior" sweat lodge retreat has filed a lawsuit against the organizer of the event, self-help guru James Arthur Ray.

The suit, which was filed on October 30, came a day after the family of one of the three people who died filed a similar suit in Coconino County Superior Court.

Sidney Spencer claims that Ray, along with unnamed employees, were negligent in not letting participants leave the sweat lodge when they became uncomfortable, and that he and the employees intimidated people into staying in the lodge despite the heat and fumes.

The suit claims that Ray "ignored [Spencer] even after she lost consciousness in the sweat lodge" and failed to provide her with timely medical care. Spencer is also claiming that Ray conducted the ceremony without a licensed health provider and failed to install a temperature-monitoring device.

Reports of the incident from survivors claim that Ray sat in the door of the sweat tent and kept people from leaving, despite knowing that people were falling ill and asking to leave.

After the incident, Ray left Sedona without talking to police and returned to his home in California, where he continued conducting his self-help seminars and events. However, last week, Ray seemed to have a change in heart and announced he would be postponing all events to focus on finding out what caused the tragedy in Sedona.[6]

Personal Responsibility

There will be more lawsuits. As of this writing, Ray has been charged with three counts of manslaughter. Will he be found guilty? You'll probably know that answer by the time you're reading this book. You can count on a lot of "piling on," to use a common expression. But let this be a signal: *You are always responsible for you!* Medical professionals have been known to make mistakes, and patients who have acted on their advice have sometimes died. Clergymen have seduced the innocent with lies only to be hidden from the public for years by their colleagues. There are many more instances of deceit, both intentional and unknowing. The message again is this: Take responsibility for the proverbial me, myself, and I.

Perhaps the toxicology reports will reveal some substance in the hot coals, in the tent material or its patches, or in something else that may explain the deaths despite the best and most responsible efforts on behalf of the victims. That said, the questions remain: *What if I give away my power to some guru or other authority figure, and then something bad happens? Do I have a personal responsibility for whatever occurs?*

What if you trust another blindly with your life, your spirituality, or your belief system—do you have any responsibility if everything you believe is wrong? What if you thought for a moment and realized that you had indeed given away your power by taking the word of someone or some group and never truly investigated it for yourself? Would you do anything about it? Would you change anything? Could you?

chapter 7

The Meaning of It All

"Millions long for immortality who do not know what to do with themselves on a rainy Sunday afternoon."

— SUSAN ERTZ

What if you discovered that there was no afterlife, no purpose—that everything ended when the brain wound down and the lights went out? Does it matter? The Australian evangelist James Duffecy, said: "A dead atheist is someone who is all dressed up with no place to go." Have you given this any real thought?

When we're young, we feel bulletproof. Life is full, and death is something in the faraway future. "Who wants to live to be old anyway?" is the question most young people respond with when asked about their thoughts on life and death. Of course the counter to this question is: "Who wants to live to be 100? Just ask anyone who is 99."

When I was a very young man, the words of the American poet Henry Wadsworth Longfellow were burned indelibly into my mind:

And our hearts, though stout and brave,
Still, like muffled drums, are beating
Funeral marches to the grave.

Not long ago, I decided to invest some serious inquiry into the notion of the survival of personal consciousness beyond death. I had two questions: First, is there evidence beyond a reasonable doubt that personal consciousness survives the grave? Second, would I do anything differently if I concluded that there was no life after death? Would you make any changes if you knew that when it was over, it was "dust to dust" for you and me?

In undertaking any inquiry of this nature, it's worth remembering the words of Albert Einstein: "No problem can be solved from the same level of consciousness that created it." However, in order to proceed, let's take these questions in order and, in the process, allow me to add some background.

Beyond a Reasonable Doubt

For years I was a practicing criminalist. During that period, I ran lie-detection tests and conducted investigations. I built cases and provided courtroom testimony on both civil and criminal matters. For me, the method used by our judicial system to get at the truth is as valid as any method that exists—not that there aren't mistakes, for there are many. Still, when we examine the nature of the burden of proof for any so-called form of knowing, it's hard to find a better system than the one used by our courts.

If our justice system is good enough to decide the fate of a human being, even in life-and-death situations, is it not good enough to weigh the evidence for something like life *after* death? Can we borrow this method to pursue the evidence, treating it as though it were a case before a court of law? I think so, for when we seriously inquire into whether personal consciousness survives the grave, the evidence that can be brought to make a case should be weighed for reasonableness.

Science argues with itself as much as philosophy does, and neither provides a means for knowing absolutely. Indeed, the so-called epistemological certainty that does emerge is the sureness of *un*certainty. In other words, in philosophical parlance, the only thing we can be assured of is that certainty doesn't exist; and even if it did, we couldn't be positive about it.

How Can You Know?

If you can't know for sure, how then can you know? How could you ever answer questions such as: Are the reports of life after death such as near-death experiences and reincarnation data culturally relevant? That is, do you see and experience according to your expectations, your cultural and/or religious biases? What are the current philosophical and scientific positions on the matter? Is it possible to assemble enough evidence to demonstrate mathematically, well beyond a matter of chance, that life after death is probable? Is there a description possible for what to expect on the other side, if there is an other side? Is it possible to draw any conclusions regarding the matter? What do the cynics, agnostics, and atheists believe? Why has faith in spiritual matters become unscientific? Why are so many young people enamored with the arguments of some, such as Richard Dawkins, who use science as the new religion?[1]

Obviously, there are answers to these questions, even if those answers entail admitting the possibility of uncertainty.

Greek philosopher Zeno of Elea showed in a famous paradox that the Greek warrior Achilles could never catch a tortoise.[2] In doing so, he demonstrated that pure logic can be fallible, since common sense and observation of life tell us that this paradox could not hold up in the real world—clearly Achilles, or even a small child, could overtake a tortoise. Logic has its place, but so does our own examination of the situation. We make decisions every day based on the information available, even when the questions are difficult. Some of those are indeed life-and-death decisions.

You might fairly ask, "With all the books out there on death, dying, and the afterlife, why are we examining that question here?" The answer is both simple and complex.

What Difference Does It Make?

First, and most simply, does it matter to you if there's no afterlife? I mean, how would you behave if you learned, or had reason to believe, that the bumper sticker motto "Life sucks and then you die" is true—true at all levels, as in dead, dead, dead, no afterlife? On the other hand, what if you were an atheistic or agnostic juror in our hypothetical trial and you found that the evidence for an afterlife was confirmed beyond a reasonable doubt? Would you change your conduct?

In other words, what if you believed in reincarnation because you read a book about Bridey Murphy (an Irishwoman whom an American housewife claimed she had been in a past life), but now you hear that much of the information associated with that famous case has been debunked, shown to be false, or otherwise explained. What then? What if on top of that you read *Fads & Fallacies in the Name of Science,* by Martin Gardner, and discovered that this entire area of inquiry is fraught with misrepresentation, false pretense, and outright fraud. Indeed, when you finished Gardner's work, you might feel intellectually foolish for ever entertaining such an idea as the supernatural or life after death.

Universal Values

Second, the more complicated answer has to do with the meaning of life and whether or not some universal value system possibly exists. The code generally embraced in today's culture is one of cultural relativity. Whatever is right for the people in XYZ country is fine for them, and whatever is right for us is fine for us. Viewed from this perspective, some of today's most troubling questions can't be answered. The word *right* itself is wrong. *Right* is only a value judgment and means absolutely nothing about reality per se, as philosopher Edmund Husserl and his student Martin Heidegger might say. Is there then such a thing as a universal value, such as the one I posed earlier: "All life is sacred"?

There are many ways to get to a value system, including those under the general auspices of secular humanism. Unfortunately, none of them can provide the rigor that might arise out of "knowing" that there's a purpose to life, for there can be no purpose if there is no afterlife. Alternatively, if there's no meaning per se, if life is just a one-time go around, then the question remains: *How would you live differently if you "knew" that to be true?* Either way, the inquiry takes on a life of its own as soon as you open your mind to accepting either possibility or, for that matter, rejecting both.

Consciousness as a Radio Wave

What would rejecting both options mean? There are many possibilities, most of which are beyond the scope of this book. Consider this, however: What if your consciousness survives as a radio wave might? That is, imagine that your every thought was broadcast as an energetic form from your head into some sphere that collected, agglomerated, and stored everyone's thoughts. Imagine further that, by electromagnetic means or simple mental procedures, you could somehow call upon this field of information like a radio receiver tuning in to a station. The folks who'd had the thoughts might be long dead, and yet their ideas aren't—at least in this scenario. If you assume that this kind of personal-consciousness survival is the only continuation beyond the grave, then both of the original ideas (life beyond death and no life beyond death) are null. In that case, this scenario may well give rise to a change in behavior. Perhaps you choose to read or think more so that your thoughts are rich and, you hope, will benefit future generations.

My Experiences

So is there evidence beyond a reasonable doubt for life after death? I've had experiences that definitely argue for it. I've seen so-called ghosts in my home; at least, I saw them or they were some figment of my imagination. I've smelled the presence of my best friend after he passed away. In fact, I frequently smelled him for a couple of years after his passing. He'd been burned over a large part of his body during World War II, which led to a unique and highly distinguishable body odor.

I've also had experiences that point toward an afterlife. That said, I know only too well how easy it is to get carried away with one's imagination. Where the world of the paranormal and the world of imagination meet is often a very fine seam. I remember, for example, visiting a client's home years ago when I was an undergraduate. The man was a taxidermist, and when we were finished with our business, he wanted to show me his work, so we descended into his basement. There I found every conceivable creature staring at me with large eyes, no matter where they were positioned in the room. The entire thing gave me the willies. I was, however, polite and complimentary. He was obviously a very skilled taxidermist, but I couldn't keep scenes from the movie *Psycho* out of my head.

It was very late when I left my client's home. I had a date that evening, and I was more than an hour late. I drove a 1968 Mercury Cougar at the time, and it was one mean vehicle. When I first got into the car, I sensed something or someone in the backseat. It startled me, so I quickly stepped out again. I looked for something in the back—a small space was all this two-door sports car had room for—but there was nothing there. I brushed the feeling off, got back in, and started the car. Down the highway I went, but the sensation came back strongly. As I approached a very well-lit major intersection at about 11 P.M. with no traffic in sight, I slammed on the brakes and jumped out the instant the car stopped. There, with the driver's door wide open—dome light on, under the bright streetlights—I looked in my car. This time I examined the back even more carefully. There was nothing on the floorboards and nothing on the seats. The car was empty.

I felt stupid. I got back into the driver's seat and drove to my date's home. I parked alongside the front curb of her home on a dead-end street and stepped out of the Cougar. As I did so, a cat squealed a high-pitched scream and bolted out of the back of my car, running past me or between my feet—I don't know which to this day. I stood for a moment staring at my car and thinking about the feeling I'd had. Where could this cat have been? I looked up the way I'd driven in, which was where the cat had run. There was no cat, but there was a very tall man in a long black trench coat moving away from me down the sidewalk. Where had he come from? The whole matter spooked me, so I went up to the house. Once inside, I relaxed, put the issue out of my mind, and got on with my life. In retrospect, however, perhaps I should have attempted to speak with the stranger in the street.

Just where does imagination end and the paranormal begin, or is there really only imagination? The way to know is to investigate.

The Investigation

In order to proceed with my investigation into the possibility of an afterlife, I decided to go straight to the horse's mouth. Beginning in 2009, I used my radio show to contact and interview guests who had firsthand experiences with it. Knowledge of a whole host of areas could be admitted as evidential. They included experiences, séances, reincarnation, shamans, psychics and psychic phenomena, miracles, faith healers, out-of-body experiences (OBEs), ectoplasm and other manifestations, and more. I heard stories from health-care professionals about near-death experiences (NDEs) that gave me chills. I listened to electronic-voice phenomena (EVPs) and heard relevant recorded answers from the other side. I investigated reincarnation stories that were of a much higher caliber than the Bridey Murphy tale, and so on.

When I was finished, two things were clear to me. First, there should be a book based on the available evidence of an afterlife, so I gave the idea to a writer friend and a documentary film producer. Second, if I were a juror in this case, the evidence definitely met the beyond-a-reasonable-doubt or "BARD" rule.

A Purpose to Life

What does that say? Does it mean that spirits linger around just to provide evidence or something silly like that? Of course not. What it suggests to me is that there's a purpose to life because an afterlife exists.

If you don't believe there's any such thing, what would it take to convince you otherwise? Is it possible for you to change your mind? If you believe there's an afterlife, what would it take to convince you that there's a universal purpose behind it—one that implies a universal notion of right and wrong?

If you can accept this possibility, what do you think the first principle of right and wrong is or should be? Do you believe all life is sacred, or do you qualify what you think of as life and under what circumstances it's sacred? What if your beliefs were all wrong? Would it make any difference in how you live? Does knowing that life survives death—that is, that personal consciousness continues beyond the grave—dictate anything with respect to how you conduct yourself? What if there is no afterlife?

chapter 8

Pets and an Afterlife

"All our knowledge merely helps us to die a more painful death than the animals that know nothing."

— MAURICE MAETERLINCK

The idea that animals know nothing is disconcerting to me, because I know better. I've had the good fortune to live with animals all my life. My parents used to tell me about how our German shepherd, Queen, taught me to walk. According to the story, I would hold on to her and raise myself up, and then she would slowly walk while I held on to her back and hair.

People tend to do two things with respect to animals. If it's their pet, they anthropomorphize nearly everything about it. The pet thinks, converses with them, has an afterlife, is their devoted friend, understands them in ways no one else can, and so forth. If the animal is one chosen for the table, then it's a dumb beast without any sense of self. It was given to humans to eat; after all, it's written that man was given dominion over the beasts of the earth.

Ferdinand

In some cultures, horses are a delicacy, and people eat them. Our smaller pets, such as dogs, are often fed horse meat via commercial foods. The great racehorse Ferdinand, who won the 112th Kentucky Derby, was later killed for his flesh. This beloved champion, ridden by hall of fame jockey Billy Shoemaker to capture the crown, ended up at a slaughterhouse in Japan.

According to Margaret Baird of the Humane Society: "Ferdinand earned a then-record of $609,500 in winnings [from the Derby alone], but the colt wasn't through. After finishing second in the Preakness and third in the Belmont Stakes in 1986, the thoroughbred found his winning stride again the following season and won Horse of the Year honors by nosing out 1987 Kentucky Derby winner Alysheba in the Breeders' Cup Classic."[1]

Why did such a regal animal end up in a slaughterhouse? Breeders will tell you that Ferdinand wasn't a great stud, so his utility was limited once he could no longer earn money. I guess the logic went something like this: if he can't pay his feed bill, why feed him?

How do you feel about that? I, for one, am disgusted, but the Japanese owners were applying different criteria to the value of an animal's life than I would.

Boss

I love horses, so the idea of eating them is akin to eating my dog or cat. Still, with that said, I once raised a young dairy bull calf by hand, and it followed me like a puppy. When it was a healthy and fattened seven- or eight-month-old, I sent it to slaughter. I'll never forget the thud in my stomach when that calf bellowed at me as though it knew it was in trouble, a sound I'd grown familiar with from raising it. Anthropomorphize—I suppose that's exactly what I did.

I thought, *This calf I called Boss is asking, "What did I do wrong?"* He did nothing wrong. I was just blind to what was happening because it was the custom at my horse ranch every year to obtain, tie off, feed, fatten, and kill dairy bull calves. "Custom"—how much are we blind to because of custom?

Animal Consciousness

I've seen some remarkable displays of animal consciousness. I've watched goats adopt newborn foals that have lost their mothers. I've seen horses instantly know when one of their stable mates dies and, in unison, sound out what I think of as their cries of good-bye.

I carried my best friend to the veterinarian to be put down due to an incurable and painful disease, and I swelled with anger when the veterinary assistant blew the main artery in my friend's leg and caused her extra pain—a last whimper in the process. I watched her eyes as she passed, her head in my lap and my tears falling on her face.

I've seen that look of love and felt the agony of separation. I could recount many stories of the consciousness of animals, but I've already told many in my book *What Does That Mean?* Here, my interest is different.

Sense of Self

Our rather arbitrary demarcation between a life worth saving and one that's not is remarkably stupid, but we're blind to it for the most part. Researchers have identified a number of animals that have a sense of self. A scientist paints a red spot on an orangutan. When the animal sees itself in the mirror, it will immediately attempt to wipe the color from itself and may even check its hands to see if it has been successful at removing any of the red.[2] Other animals have demonstrated self-recognition, including elephants.[3] If animals are self-aware, if they can communicate, if they feel pain, how do we sort them according to the ones we eat and the ones we cherish as friends?

Think back to the BARD standard. In my investigation, I included animals. Do they have an afterlife? Imagine the next scenario, based on a story told to me by Kim Sheridan, author of *Animals and the Afterlife*.

Animal Psychic

You've lost your pet. You've had this animal since it was a very young puppy, barely six weeks old. It was a small dog, so it slept on your bed, lay at your feet while you were sitting in your rocking chair, nuzzled up to you in front of the winter fires that burned on the hearth, licked your face when you were feeling ill, brought your slippers, played endless hours of fetch, and much more. Imagine how close you might feel to this friend, always there and always faithful to you.

After 14 years, your friend passes. You're distraught. You think you can never own another dog, crying when you're alone and thinking of your companion. Then one day you hear of a psychic who speaks to animals that have died. You find this information both unbelievable and unforgettable. For days you think about calling this person, and then one day you do.

When she arrives for your appointment, the psychic tells you all about your lost loved one. Although what you hear makes you feel good, you still doubt the veracity of the information. Finally, you blurt out, speaking directly to your friend, "Tell me something that only you and I could know! I need to know that it's really you."

The psychic is still for moment, then she looks you in the eye and says, "Do you remember that old teddy bear you used to keep in your rocking chair? The one you used to sit with? Well, I was jealous, so I took it outside through the pet door and buried it under that big old rose bush you avoided because of its humongous thorns."

You're stunned for a moment. Then, as though someone waved a wand, you're up and at it with a shovel digging around the old rose bush. What do you find? That old teddy bear.

Do you still doubt the authenticity of what the psychic has been telling you?

If this scenario or others like it were actually to happen, would you think differently about animals? The truth is, not only has it happened once, it has happened many times. One researcher I interviewed, the previously mentioned Kim Sheridan, has documented thousands of cases demonstrating that animals do indeed have an afterlife.[4]

Okay, maybe you say, "I can buy that with dogs and cats; but what about pigs, sheep, cows, and the like?" Where do you draw the line?

Transmigration

I suppose if you live in an environment in which you're totally dependent upon animals for your sustenance, then you must do what's necessary to survive, albeit with great respect, I hope. But what if there's any truth to animal transmigration? What if you discovered that your deceased loved ones could come back as animals to befriend you and aid you in some way? Would you be like some in India who'd starve before they slaughtered and ate a cow? What defines a reasonable belief?

This book is about all of us and our self-discovery, even if what we discover includes more uncertainty. Charles R. Magel, professor of philosophy at Moorhead University, put the entire problem this way: Ask the experimenters why they experiment on animals, and the answer is: "Because the animals are like us." Ask the experimenters why it's morally okay to experiment on animals, and the answer is: "Because the animals aren't like us."

Animal experimentation rests on a logical contradiction. I would add that our entire understanding of animals relies on similar dissonance. What do you think? What if your ideas about animals were all wrong? Would you—could you—do anything about it? If not, why not?

chapter 9

Crime and Punishment

*"If he has a conscience he will suffer for his mistake.
That will be punishment—as well as the prison."*

— FYODOR DOSTOEVSKY

Do you have a conscience? Does your neighbor have one? Are they the same? How about the person in Yemen who's training to bomb Americans—does he or she have a conscience? Is this a thing built by society and its norms? What did Dostoevsky mean when he spoke of the prison imposed by the conscience?[1]

Is guilt a part of your conscience? What if your sense of right and wrong is only a product of societal norms? What if those standards are awfully wrong? Stephen R. Covey, author of the best-selling book *The 7 Habits of Highly Effective People*, says: "Every human has four endowments—self-awareness, conscience, independent will, and creative imagination. These give us the ultimate human freedom . . . the power to choose, to respond, to change."

Can you change your conscience? Do your moral sensibilities impinge on your so-called independent will?

Does will mean willpower? Or is it your inner identification of who you are and what you choose to do? Or is it both of these . . . and more?

Who are you? Are you the product of your socialization? Of course. Are you a product of the experiences you've had and how you've interpreted them? Yes, again. Are you your body? That, too, but at the same time, you're also not your physicality. Think of this: every cell in your body is different from the cells that made you when you were two years old. From the perspective of continuity, you're still the same person that you were as a toddler; but you're also not the same, at least from the standpoint of your body.

Beam Me Up, Scotty

Think back to the idea of the mind in the computer. Another way to approach this problem is one I call the "Beam me up, Scotty" scenario. Imagine that you're about to make a journey from one planet to another via a transporter. Your wife has made this journey many times, and she assures you that everything will be just fine. Despite this, you remain uneasy. The device scans you, registering and recording every molecule, every atom, every aspect of your being, including your memory, consciousness, and so forth. When it's energized, you—or more accurately, your image, the information that is you—are transported like a fax. You're faxed from one destination to another. Rather, a perfect copy of you arrives at the destination planet; and at the moment of energizing, the you in the local transporter is destroyed.

You arrive at your destination and step out of the transporter. You feel in every way that this is you. You've just arrived—but what if something goes wrong? What if your local body isn't destroyed? So there you are in two places.

Now what if you're told that something went wrong, and the local you will die of heart failure in a day or two, but not to worry. The you at the end destination is fine, and that you will go on and frolic with your wife and children. Does that give you comfort? Not for me—not in the least! How about for you?

Your Programming

Now imagine that you learn that every thought you have comes from deep in your unconscious. Not only that, but all of the programming you've received has led to very predictable outcomes—so much so that your every action could easily be considered predetermined. In other words, your programming has now been sorted out by computers with vast capabilities—machines that actually look into your brain and, through various outcome-oriented studies, accurately map your responses to different stimuli. Like any computer, your total input from friends, family, experiences, genes, ideas, behaviors, styles, and more has programmed you to respond in certain ways. Where you think you're making a choice, you are indeed only acting out a predetermined pattern.

To make this more credible, realize that much of scientific research suggests just such a situation. There are strong links between criminality and genetics, and between subconscious scripts and behavior—connections that all suggest that given sufficient information and computing power, they could predict your every action.[2, 3, 4]

Who's Responsible?

So here you are, aware that everything you might do today or tomorrow is already written somewhere. Are you responsible for anything you do? Is anyone, given this proposition?

Oscar Wilde said: "Nothing makes one so vain as being told one is a sinner. Conscience makes egotists of us all." Are we egotistical to think that we have a conscience and that it instructs as to right and wrong, punishes us for bad behavior, and leaves us alone if we do things right? Is Wilde on to something here? Clearly, if we believe that we can choose differently, as Covey insists, then we can also claim responsibility for our actions—good and bad. But what if we're merely under the illusion that this is so?

Research shows us that the conscious mind has a basic need to assume control—to be in charge. When subjects make decisions on the basis of unknown subliminal input, they nevertheless make up a reason for the choice. In fact, research has further shown that as much as one-third of the normal population will develop pathological symptoms in their "rational process of trying to make sense of unexplained sources of arousal."[5]

Making Sense of the World

The fact is that in our modern culture, we're all processing ambiguous and unknown or unidentified sources of arousal all the time; and while this is going on, our minds are consciously searching for sources and making up stories to provide us with the kind of continuity that we find comforting. We ask ourselves why we did something, and the mind provides us with a reason.

So if you were one of the men on that somewhat dangerous bridge I described earlier, your answer to why you felt attracted to the young woman who was working on some psychology project will have many possibilities. None of them, however, is likely to include the fact that you were aroused by the danger and not the woman—that you just transferred that arousal to her.

Nature and Nurture

What if we learned that every action by a human being is predetermined by the nature-nurture impact at an early age? Imagine some criminal behavior. Let's say that an escaped convict, fleeing from police officers, runs into a neighborhood home. There he finds an older couple peacefully having dinner at their small kitchen table. The husband stands up and demands to know what the criminal is doing in their home and, at the same time, orders him to leave. The escapee sees the fork in the home owner's hand as a weapon and shoots him, killing the older man instantly. The wife runs to her husband's side, kneeling next to his dead body, and then stands and rages at the murderer with her fists flying. He strikes her on the head with his gun, and she, too, falls dead to the floor.

You're a member of the jury, and you hear the facts of the case. Then you hear how this man was programmed by his upbringing and his genetic makeup. Do you absolve him of the crime because he really didn't "will" it? He had no real choice, after all. Or do you hold him accountable? If you choose the latter, don't you have to take preventive measures and lock up everyone who has a genetic or nurture-based predisposition to commit a crime? If the technical ability exists to screen everyone and more or less accurately separate the criminals-to-be from the good citizens, then don't you do the screening and imprison the dangerous ones on a preventive basis?

It's a slippery slope either way. Most normal people have the ability to be bad, truly evil, as you saw earlier when learning about the Lucifer Effect. Obviously, you can't jail everyone. That said, nearly every human being also has the potential to do genuinely helpful things for other members of society. So if you knew the criminals before they caused harm, would you want them imprisoned? And if the perpetrators were made this way, how could you justify holding them accountable for their actions?

Mitigating Circumstances

We take many shortcuts in our best efforts to mete out justice. One of those shortcuts has to do with the notion of *free will*. But if will isn't really free, how can someone be blamed for an act of even the most vile nature? Yet that's exactly what we do. Our criminal courts allow for mitigating factors, so we have defenses for the insane, the temporarily insane, and so forth.

But what if we discover that behavior is indeed pre-determined—what defense is there for that? Should there be one?

There's no easy answer for these *What if?* quandaries. What's left is an awareness that within our simplistic way of doing things are many loopholes that have gone unnoticed, unreconciled, and largely ignored.

Should we do anything about this? Can we do anything about this? What do you think? What if you had the power to change any of it—what would you do?

chapter 10

The Dream Within the Dream

"The greatest obstacle to discovering the shape of the earth, the continents, and the oceans was not ignorance but the illusion of knowledge."

— DANIEL J. BOORSTIN

Are you awake? It seems like a simple question, but think about it for a minute. What is meant by *awake?* Are you awake when you're dreaming? How about when you're having a lucid dream—where you become aware that you're dreaming—don't you have some state of alertness then? Are there stages of wakefulness? When you see a small child throwing a tantrum over silly nothings, do you consider the child to be fully awake? Is a mature mind-set more awake?

Is it possible that we're the figment of someone else's dream, as René Descartes once reasoned?[1] Perhaps we're dreaming within another's reverie—a dream within a dream. Maybe the Creator is sleeping or imagining in some kind of daydream, and we're figments of that. Could we wake up within the dream?

When Jesus said, "Let those with ears hear and those with eyes see," was he speaking about a differentiated level of wakefulness? [2] When you write your name automatically, are you as awake as when you monitor every muscle movement of that otherwise reflexive gesture? Can you be too awake? When you do carefully pay attention to exactly how you sign your name, you'll find that you actually impede the process. Are states of automatic consciousness less awake than attentive states? In other words, is attention a component of wakefulness and, if so, is it necessarily so?

Driving on Automatic

You can probably relate to the idea of driving down the freeway with some time passing while you're deep in thought. Suddenly, you realize that you're approaching your exit, and you snap out of that "spaced out" state. Leaving your automatic driving mode behind, you take back full control of your automobile. How do you describe this kind of wakefulness that falls short of automatic and therefore isn't fully attentive? Is attention necessary to be fully awake?

There's an old story about the Buddha that goes something like this:

> The Buddha is traveling one day when he meets a stranger on the road. The stranger falls to his knees before the Buddha and states, "You must be a god."
>
> The Buddha answers, "No, my friend. I am not a god."

The stranger says, "Well, then you must be a demigod."
Again the Buddha speaks: "No, I am not a demigod."
The frustrated stranger then looks up at the Buddha
and asks, "Then tell me: What are you?"
The Buddha replies, "Awake."

What kind of wakefulness is that? Are there levels of awareness that relate to spiritual life? Maturity does bear on our ability to discern, and typically adjusted adults no longer throw themselves on the floor kicking and wailing in full-blown tantrums, so wakefulness must also include a degree of maturity.

Waking Up

For years I've championed the idea that people wake up a little bit at a time. In fact, for more than 25 years, I've dedicated my work and research to that proposition through my company, Progressive Awareness Research. The name obviously shows my bias. So exactly how do people wake up, if that's an appropriate metaphor to use?

Think a moment about your own life. Have there been times when you lost control, perhaps out of anger, and your temper took control of the moment? Have there been other instances when you were able to remain calm and collected and win the day through effective persuasion, or when you just let the matter go as not that important—not worth a major fight?

What in yourself was different when you lost control from when you didn't? Usually the answer can't only be an age difference, for matters of this kind can and do occur at all stages of life. So what sets the two occasions apart?

A State of Mind

I suggest that the difference is a state of mind. In one case, you operate reactively, and in the other, you're more proactive. Reactive thinking and action is automatic. You "go off," and then you think about it, to borrow a metaphor from William James (whose theory was that you see a bear, run, and then become afraid).[3] In this reactive/automatic stage, you aren't attending to a rational set of data; rather, you're responding from conditioned and emotional information.

Here's something really important to note about your self-examination: there's seldom a real data match with the response when you're reactive. Let me say that again: the data, or stimulus, for losing your temper is seldom a match for the real reason you become angry (which is the conditioned data).

Let's pursue that for a moment. Think back to a time as an adult when you became very upset. Perhaps someone said something to you, and you took it to be disrespectful or a challenge or an attack. Now think of what triggered the event. Did the catalyst match your conclusion? The thing about conditioned emotional triggers is that they usually aren't rational, logical, straightforward, linear, cause-and-effect events. We lash out and then later recognize that we were "over the top," to use a colloquial phrase.

Advanced stages of reactive thinking, which I view as nonthinking, are exemplified by such events as road rage. The cause is never sufficient provocation for the action that follows. The disproportionate response is an extreme example of the disconnect in the data match. Obviously, the party acting out road rage is less awake than, say, the pope, or hopefully a clinical psychologist or any other health-care professional.

Context

Our purpose here isn't to examine road rage or even data matches per se. Instead, we're examining what it means to be awake and, thereby, what it means to be asleep. It's easy enough to see that there are varying degrees of wakefulness. I think we can also conclude at this point that everyone, including ourselves, knows these different states in varying environments or contexts. So in one instance, we're able to ignore stimuli that might set us off in other situations.

For example, think of what actions are acceptable in a public place versus in your home. Extend this to all arenas of life and I'm sure you'll discover that you're different people in different circumstances. In one context, a swear word is taken in jest; and in another, it's insulting. Your co-worker can say things to you at the office that you'd challenge if they were spoken in front of your children in your own home. In one situation, you allow a police officer to address you harshly about your speeding. In another—say, presiding at a public bond hearing—you don't tolerate the same tone from a testifying officer.

Okay, so we have different waking states. How do we define wakefulness? Is it just a matter of always being alert to our thoughts and their influence over our actions? Or does it include a level of learning?

Justice

Let's assume in this thought experiment that you're an awake person living in an environment that's governed by a form of Sharia or Islamic law. A teenager steals a loaf of bread to feed his younger brother, and the law says you cut his hand off. You're an awake person—but what are you awake to? If you're awake to your culture and the many reasons and teachings behind its legal system, then you support the law. If, however, you're awake to the system known in the Western world, you find the punishment much harsher than the crime. In your Western mind-set, you want the punishment to fit the crime. Is one of these views more awake than the other?

Imagine that you're in power, and as a result, you can choose what happens to this teenager. You decide to go with your Western mind-set and sentence the thief to community service. You give him a broom and assign him to sweep the streets for a period of time. Your conscience feels good, the baker gets his loaf of bread back, and society is compensated by having clean streets.

Now imagine that as the thief sweeps, he also cases some of the homes and businesses along the street. He's less fearful of punishment at this point, since he still has two hands, and after all, sweeping isn't the end of the world. After one week of clean-up duty, the thief decides that he has sufficiently observed the routines of the people living in the area, so he breaks into a home that appears to belong to a wealthy family. Once inside, he comes upon a young teenage boy who has been home ill all week. The boy screams for help, so the thief takes the crowbar he used to pry open the door and slams it against the boy's head. The child falls dead to the floor.

The teenaged thief is back in court, and again, you have the power. Had you cut his hand off—the very hand he used to kill the boy—that child would still be alive. Add this to your thought experiment: the dead boy was your son. What level of law do you want enacted now? Are you less awake because of it? Would you have been more awake to have enforced the existing law in the first place and cut off the thief's hand?

Wakefulness

Typically, behavioral researchers think of wakefulness as having to do with the difference between automatic and thoughtful processes. As human beings, we all take certain mental shortcuts, and many of them are both appropriate and necessary. That is, there's no reason to invest conscious energy in tasks that can be performed automatically with as much—or even more—ease and safety, as by attending to their every minute detail. Signing your name is just one example of a case where it's more efficient to allow the process to be automatic.

Still, there are a variety of ways in which we can fail ourselves by not attending to some sides of our mental life. Our judgments can be skewed by unconscious automatic processes, which render us vulnerable to arriving at false conclusions. In his book *The Mindful*

Brain, author Daniel Siegel defines mindfulness in this way: "A useful fundamental view is that mindfulness can be seen to consist of the important dimensions of the self-regulation of attention and a certain orientation to experience . . . 'a particular orientation toward one's experience in the present moment, an orientation that is characterized by curiosity, openness and acceptance.'"[4]

Thinking about Thinking

In other words, we should be thinking about our thinking if we're to avoid reactive responses. Can we become more awake by doing this, which Siegel refers to as *metacognition?*[5] Is there any other way we can become more awake? I think not—what do you think? Have you thought about this before? Can you stop a reactive impulse if you're unaware of it? Can you break a reactive habit or pattern if you practice metacognition? What if you learned you weren't as awake as you could be—what would you do? How much time and energy would you dedicate to waking up? What if you thought you were already fully awake—would you have anything left to learn?

Thinking about thinking may be our only way to wake up. I love how Siegel describes the automatic thinker, the person who is more or less asleep:

> For some people, this "living on automatic" is a routine way of life. If our attention is on something other than what we are doing for most of our lives we can come to feel empty and numb. As automatic thinking dominates our subjective sense of the world, life becomes repetitive and dull. Instead of experience

having an emergent feeling of fresh discovery, as a child sensing the world for the first time, we come to feel dead inside, "dead before we die."[6] Siegel summarizes: "A cascade of reinforcing mindlessness can create a world of thoughtless interactions, cruelty and destruction."[7]

Living Awake

Being awake is something that everyone capable of reading is able to do. We have some 10,000 synaptic connections linking over 100 billion neurons, all of which could carry information at any moment—yet as staggering as that might seem, we still have the ability to monitor our thoughts and think about our thinking. By listening carefully to our stream of consciousness, our own inner talk, we can also observe hidden agendas that exist in our subconscious. In that way, we can gain access to more of our own mind and behavior. We're capable of knowing that the vile spit in the glass in front of us isn't so vile after all, since we just spat it there.

If you're unfamiliar with this metaphor, let me expand on this. Think of the spit in your mouth. As saliva, it's good and you're grateful for it; however, if you spit it into a glass and think about drinking it right back, you discover that it suddenly becomes repugnant. Why? Some would argue context conditioning, and I am one of those people.

But the important point here is that our mental shortcut (pulling information from previous categories—also called *heuristics*) fails to identify the different context, and thus our decision is predisposed by automatic processes. In this way, we make many choices, and some of them just aren't the best idea for anyone concerned. In my book *Choices and Illusions,* I consider many examples of these shortcut errors that fail us in both the short and the long run.[8]

What if we decided to evaluate this idea of being awake? What then? It's up to you—what will you do?

chapter 11

A Rich Inner Life

*"Today, the degradation of the inner life is
symbolized by the fact that the only place sacred
from interruption is the private toilet."*

— LEWIS MUMFORD

What is a rich inner life? Is it as the *Sri Guru Granth
Sahib* (the holy book of the Sikhs) puts it: "The Divine
Light of the Infinite Lord, who owns the soul and the
breath of life, is deep within the inner being"? Is it as
Einstein is often quoted as saying?

Strange is our situation here upon earth. Each of us
comes for a short visit, not knowing why, yet sometimes
seeming to a divine purpose. From the standpoint of
daily life, however, there is one thing we do know: That
we are here for the sake of others . . . for the countless
unknown souls with whose fate we are connected by
a bond of sympathy. Many times a day, I realize how
much my outer and inner life is built upon the labors of
people, both living and dead, and how earnestly I must
exert myself in order to give in return as much as I have
received.

Imagination

Is a rich inner life dependent upon serving others, or is it just one full of imaginary people and places? To have a rich inner life, do I need a rich imagination? If people have very limited ways of visualizing or simply cannot do so, does that mean their inner lives lack the richness of those who see everything with their mind's eye in living color? What is a rich inner life to you? What if you discovered that yours was a barren desert? What if you learned that to have a full inner life, you needed to tend a garden of sorts, to build an oasis within you?

Let's use some imagination and do another thought experiment. Imagine that you watched a television program in which a hypnotist who specialized in past-life regression explained that he had uncovered three worlds in his work. One is this realm, Earth. In another, everyone flies; and the third is aquatic, where all inhabitants swim. The evidence shown in the TV special is compelling, but only one side of the issue is presented. You think about what has been suggested, and you remember the hypnotist saying how common it was for people in this world—Earth—to have dreams of flying or living in an aquatic environment. You've often had both types of dreams. You ask yourself, *Does this mean I'm having memories of a past life where I did fly or swim?*

Life as a Dolphin

You go to bed and dream that you're a dolphin, and you and your extended family and your local social group generally swim together. One day you notice a small boy wading into the ocean. You can see his rather large beachfront home in the background, and the light is on in the kitchen, where you can see his mother. The boy suddenly calls out, and when you glance back at him, you see he's caught in the waves and is bobbing up and down like a fishing float. You swim to him quickly and take him to shore. His mother comes running from the house, and as she approaches, you back away. She pulls him fully from the waves while you watch, and she resuscitates him. Soon he spews water from his mouth and resumes breathing. You feel good. You've saved the boy's life, and your family is proud of you.

If you awaken from the dream at this point, is your inner life richer than before?

Let's say you continue dreaming. Because you saved the boy, you feel closer to the people who live in that big house by the sea. You make it a point to swim by from time to time, and you watch the boy grow into a fine-looking young man. A dozen years later and the boy is a 17-year-old with raging hormones. One evening he has a party on the beach, and the group builds a large bon-fire. The music is loud, and the liquor flows. You recognize that the boy's parents must not be home, so you swim nearer the shore, protectively. Your younger sister swims behind you, somewhat oblivious to what's going on. Then you hear the roar of a motor as the teens fire up the family boat. Without warning, it speeds directly at you. You hurriedly move, but your sister isn't so lucky. The propellers cut into her deeply, and blood gushes from her body.

You awaken at this point. Now how do you feel? Has your inner life been enriched by this experience? Can and should dreams be behind the enrichment we seek?

Angels

What if the dream is spiritual? Bear with me a minute. Imagine you dream that your guardian angel visits you and informs you of things you've never known. You have insights that are as clear as anything you've ever understood, and you're told about the purpose behind life. When you awaken, you remember the dream, but slowly most of it disappears into that vapor that steals away so much in the early dawn. You shower and try to remember it better. You do recollect bits and pieces, but while you shower, you also fully recall—indeed, revivify—the feeling you had in the dream. This sensation is as rich as it gets, and you deeply appreciate it. Now is your inner life richer?

Demons

Imagine that you dream of demons waiting to take you upon your death. The world in which they abide is dark and gloomy—"frightening" is an absolute understatement. You try to get away, but that isn't possible. You can't escape either the circumstances or the feeling. You become aware that this is your reward for your conduct in life. You think, *If only I could have a chance to do it over—to do it right.* Just then, you awaken and sit up. Is your inner life richer now? Will this dream affect you in any way? Will you do some things differently?

Dreams for Healing

The ancient asclepiad healing centers, said to have been created by Asclepius, the Greek God of medicine and healing, were all about using dreams as a method of healing. Greek mythology is full of miraculous accounts of those seeking relief in these healing temples. It's not uncommon today for someone to have a dream and be healed as a result. Do dreams of this nature make our inner lives richer?

What can we settle upon, if anything, that defines a rich inner life? Perhaps it's everything we notice—that we pay attention to and think about. I remember cutting a beautiful red rose for my wife. At the time, we had many roses, for I've always loved them. On this day, the petals of this one blossom called to me. I lifted it and smelled the most wonderful fragrance that any single rose has ever offered me. I turned it in the sunlight of a bright new day and watched the rainbows form upon it as the light hit dewdrops clinging gingerly to the flower. I carried this rose to my wife with a good-morning kiss. She probably doesn't even remember this—but I do. Why should this one rose stand out so fully among all my memories?

Love for Another

In the last chapter, you examined the idea of being fully awake, or at least of earnestly working at waking up. When you're awake, you're not only aware of all the thoughts you have and all the feelings you hold, but also all the glorious surroundings you find yourself in. When you fully attend to a moment—any moment— it becomes an indelible memory for tomorrow. Perhaps a rich inner life comes from waking up, whether via a dream or in a normal waking state.

What if you decided to enrich your inner life? What would you do? Is it already as full as you want? I've spoken with a number of people who have undergone life-changing events, which often are all about the potential of death or the loss of a loved one. All of these individuals have informed me that the love they have for another person defines the moment. I've known this feeling, and it does give rise to a much deeper appreciation of life and the ones you care about. Reflecting on events of this nature provides internal wealth that goes beyond my ability to communicate in words. Is it love, then, that makes for a richer inner life?

Inner Adventures

My take on this leads me to conclude that a rich outer life leads to a rich inner life, and there are adventures that we can have in dream states that enhance both states of being. Perhaps it's nonsensical to make the distinction in the first place—and perhaps not.

What's your take on this? Is your inner life rich and rewarding? If it isn't, would you like it to be? What if it were? Would anything change?

What if we all had abundant internal resources? Would the world be any different? Would despair and rage be lessened? What if I'm wrong about all of this—would it make a real difference to anyone? How could we possibly promote a rich inner life for everyone in this world? What would we have to do? Where would we begin?

I put my head on my pillow at night confident that individuals out there are working to make this a better world. They have answers, and they're taking steps to wake up the people of this planet and our leaders. They're figuring out the solutions to my *What if?* questions. What if you're one of them?

◇◇◇

chapter 12

Love Thy Neighbor

"You must not kill your neighbor, whom perhaps you genuinely hate, but by a little propaganda this hate can be transferred to some foreign nation, against whom all your murderous impulses become patriotic heroism."

— BERTRAND RUSSELL

Leviticus 19:18 states, "Thou shalt not avenge, nor bear any grudge against the children of thy people, but thou shalt love thy neighbor as thyself: I am the Lord." In Matthew 7:12 we find, "Therefore all things whatsoever ye would that men should do to you, do ye even so to them: for this is the law and the prophets." Matthew 19:16–19 says:

> And, behold, one came and said unto him, Good Master, what good thing shall I do, that I may have eternal life? And he said unto him, Why callest thou me good? There is none good but one, that is, God: but if thou wilt enter into life, keep the commandments. He saith unto him, Which? Jesus said, Thou shalt do

no murder, thou shalt not commit adultery, thou shalt not steal, thou shalt not bear false witness, honour thy father and thy mother: and *thou shalt love thy neighbor as thyself* [italics added].

Confucius says: "Love thy neighbor as thyself: Do not to others what thou would not wish be done to thyself: Forgive injuries. Forgive thy enemy, be reconciled to him, give him assistance, invoke God in his behalf."

In fact, we find a rule of this sort in most of the world's religions. The Golden Rule, "Do unto others as you would have them do unto you," comes in many varieties. The Dalai Lama put it this way: "Every religion emphasizes human improvement, love, respect for others, sharing other people's suffering. On these lines every religion has more or less the same viewpoint and the same goal."

Now, as if that wouldn't be enough to encourage helping others, it also seems that your brain is set up to reward you when you go to the aid of another. In fact, it's hardwired to release feel-good chemicals when you do something as simple as make a donation. So why would anyone ignore the plights of those they could help?

Conservation

Let's do another thought experiment, one based on events that reached national attention in 2009. Imagine that you've adopted certain causes as being important to you, one of which is the condition of nature. You want to protect the environment and stop the damage being done by others who couldn't care less, including huge corporations that pollute, uncaring hunters who might endanger some species by poaching, and so on. Because of your diligence and hard work, you've been appointed to a special committee—let's say the federal Endangered Species Committee, more popularly known as "the God Squad" because of its power in these matters.

Let's imagine that your committee hears of a potentially endangered fish that lives in the waters of the Sacramento–San Joaquin Delta in California. The sudden reduction in the fish population might be the result of a three-year drought, but it may also be caused by valley farmers drawing off water for irrigation. If you shut down water being pumped to the farms, you may save the tiny fish, but the local people will be adversely affected, as will the world's food supply. The delta consists of about 250,000 acres, and your decision to stop the pumping will reduce the region's agricultural output by between $1 and $3 billion annually. Let's assume that you place a moratorium on pumping irrigation water.

Victims

Months pass, and you begin to see the effect on your neighbors. News reports show the basin turning into a dust bowl and the area residents suffering repossessions and other indignities because they can no longer pay their bills. They can't meet their families' needs, let alone their mortgages and debt payments—because of you. There's no way they could have planned for your intervention. To them, it's as if a foreign nation confiscated their livelihoods and lurked nearby, ready to seize their property as well.

What do you do? Do you stick to your guns on principle, thinking that it's just their tough luck? Or do you go down to the valley and meet with the people, talk to their children, and see the boarded-up shops in person? Are you pleased with your decision?

What if your parents' farm was involved; and they were about to lose their livelihood, property, and retirement because of some tiny fish? Is protecting this creature worth the cost?

Do you need to be a victim or be close to a victim in order to truly weigh the consequences of your decision? Remember Bernie Madoff? I pronounce his name as "made off." He was the perpetrator of a Ponzi scheme that injured many innocent people. There was a huge outcry when Madoff's racket was exposed, and the victims were informed that their life's savings, retirement funds, and more were gone. One man took it upon himself to live large at the expense of others. If you'd been one of his victims, would you be upset?

We don't tar and feather Madoff . . . because we're civilized. Still, when victims say publicly on national television that they want to kill the man, we shrug it off with a degree of understanding. And unless we're the victims, don't we more or less do the same in the conflict between the fish and the farmers?

Love Thy Neighbor

Assume that you made the decision to stop pumping irrigation water. What would it take to change your mind? Would anything dissuade you? Is that following the admonition to love thy neighbor as thyself?

People go to church every Sunday, although the number is smaller and smaller nowadays. Still, quite a sizable proportion of our American population attends worship services. There are many reasons for the fact that fewer people are actively religious today, but that issue is outside the scope of this book, at least for the moment. On Sunday (or the Sabbath, for those who worship on a different day), these people are reminded of their commitment to God. That includes the principle embodied in the Golden Rule, yet many forget their commitment as soon as they head home. Why is that? Is it a matter of not truly believing, or are they leaving these issues to others? If they can ignore a screaming woman who's being attacked outside their apartment window, as the evidence suggests and as you read about earlier, why not ignore some stupid fish and farmer conflict? Or is it more complicated than that?

The Facts of the Matter

Our thought experiment with the fish is based on a real situation. The information given above is factual. However, consider two sentences quoted in an article by Valerie Richardson in the *Washington Times*:

> "Big Ag must now learn to do more with less," campaigner Brian Smith wrote on Earthjustice.org. "The days of copious taxpayer-subsidized water exports from the Delta are coming to an end, and the idea of killing off numerous native fish species, decimating Northern California fishing communities and turning the Delta into a fetid swamp is simply not allowed under federal law."[1]

According to this portrayal, it's all about beating big business. But is it? When you get to the facts, you find that businesses both big and small are involved, and that both sides tend to exaggerate their assertions. The bottom line remains the same, however: People are suffering, farm ownership is being threatened, and food production has taken a massive hit—and for the sake of a minnow-sized fish.

We all want our environment to be protected, and we all want to love our neighbors. What do we do when those goals conflict? How do we decide which one takes priority? What if our personal food supply was dependent upon this valley? Would we still care as much about the fish? Would you feed one of the fish to a starving child?

What if the threatened species could be moved? Would we consider doing so? The farmers have been working the land for many years. What if you learned that they'd taken precautions to protect the fish? After seeing families broken apart—their land and homes taken by the banks on account of delinquent mortgages that they couldn't pay because their water was turned off to save these creatures—what if you discovered that the farmers hadn't caused the decline in fish numbers, after all? What if a few of the farmers—say, just two or three, responded to the pressure by committing suicide, as some people did after the 1929 crash on Wall Street and during the ensuing Great Depression—and then you discover the fish continue to die off anyway?

How do we know the cost of the loss of this fish? Assume they die off; species have always done that for various reasons as a normal part of how our world works. We attack and attempt to destroy certain life forms all the time, but we call them *viruses*. This shows our culture's belief that not all creatures are necessary or, for that matter, desirable. (Think back to our earlier discussion about the different standards concerning the right to life.) On the other hand, knock out a key species and that could lead to a domino effect of disastrous consequences for all of us.

A New Way of Thinking

What if you were one of the farmers instead of the champion of the environment—would you feel differently? How do you reconcile such opposition? Little things, like little fish, have the same variations inherent in them that you find in bigger things, such as the differences between average Muslims and radicalized Islamists intent on destroying the corrupt and evil Westerner. Developing strategies to settle these matters in some way short of "the victor and the vanquished" is the only way the world will ever find peace. What if it were up to you? What would you do?

My book *Choices and Illusions* exposes the failed strategy behind most of our choices.[2] We've been trained to think in terms of "either-or," and we must step back and invent new ways of reasoning. Sometimes compromises work, but often more than that is required. It may be that we should be reframing the context in order to find alternative solutions. In a world intent on all-or-nothing gambles, either-or propositions, and win-lose scenarios, the problem doesn't have an easy solution, but what if you had the power to start that process? What would you do?

Each of us participates in the world, even if only by default. As the English philosopher John Locke might have put it: "Do nothing to oppose a decision, and you've given tacit consent to the effect of that decision." The world hears of events at nearly the speed of light in this age of 24/7 newscasts. We hear, but do we do anything? Should we?

Precedents are set every day. The little fish in some farmers' canal water in a faraway place may well set the precedent that leads to a tiny wildflower overgrowing your beautiful landscaping, and in the end, owning your yard. Worse, some small Earth creature could lead to your property being condemned in order for it to be saved. And as with farmers and the fish, there would be no compensation for the loss of your land. So what's our duty to self and other people, to nature and the future, to our country and other nations—and what do we do about it?

What if you were empowered to make the final judgment? What would you decide, and why? What if you were wrong?

❖❖❖

What If There Were No Chapter 13?

chapter 14

Pursuit of Happiness

"The rub is that the pursuit of happiness, as an end in itself, tends automatically, and widely, to be replaced by the pursuit of pleasure with a consequent general softening of the fibers of will, intelligence, spirit."

— WHITTAKER CHAMBERS

In grade school, most Americans learn the words penned by Thomas Jefferson: "We hold these truths to be self-evident, that all men are created equal, that they are endowed by their Creator with certain unalienable Rights, that among these are Life, Liberty, and the pursuit of Happiness." What is the pursuit of happiness?

Innumerable people around the world would love to come to America for the opportunities that exist here, including the opportunity to pursue happiness. In doing so, folks build futures for themselves and their families. They create businesses, homes, and lives; and in short, invest in the great American dream. Is that the pursuit of happiness?

Joy

Writer Joyce Grenfell once defined the matter in this way: "There is no such thing as the pursuit of happiness, but there is the discovery of joy." Is this true? Is happiness a matter of finding joy in your life?

The Merriam-Webster Dictionary defines happiness as:

1. *obsolete:* good fortune: Prosperity.
2a. a state of well-being and contentment: Joy.
2b. a pleasurable or satisfying experience.
3. Felicity, Aptness.

In other words, happiness is a little more complex than can be explained by one simple definition or example. In reality, it's a subjective state of mind, and there are many factors that contribute to it.

Proud parents know a sense of pride and feel a reward for their sacrifices when their child wins a full scholarship to a top university. Other parents cheer and remember the hours spent shooting hoops with their son or daughter when the child sinks the winning shot. Owners of small businesses emerge from the bank with a signed copy of their loan agreement and a check for their expansion, and they celebrate with a leap of joy and shout out to all who can hear. An older man opens his eyes in the recovery room after undergoing life-threatening surgery, and his wife of 30 years smiles and feels her heart jump with joy as her eyes meet his. A small child manages to keep his bicycle upright for the first time and can't stop himself from telling everyone because he's so excited and overjoyed by his success.

These examples could go on forever, but the point is obvious. Happiness is many things to many people, and what makes us glad one moment—say, the bank loan just mentioned—may make us miserable at some other point.

The pursuit of happiness, then, would seem dependent upon the freedom to seek out that which provides our subjective joy, as long as it doesn't infringe upon another's right to do the same. Our courts have more or less settled on something close to this definition, so what happens when happiness becomes a prerogative rather than something we pursue?

The Happiness Entitlement

The happiness entitlement is what happens when society begins to expect that government will provide for every need. Once this notion is in place, then the definition of *needs* is expanded. "Spread the wealth" were the words of President Barack Obama. Is this how we pursue happiness?

Of course, a happy society is one where everyone's needs are met. Most people also have a basic desire to help those less fortunate than themselves. Why should one person have an abundance of all good things while another struggles to put food on the table? It seems, therefore, that there's merit to Obama's "spread the wealth" philosophy. Doesn't everyone deserve to be prosperous?

Deferred Gratification

What if you're an entrepreneur, struggling to make ends meet? You've been in business for 20 years, and during that time there have been lean years and good years. You look at your Social Security report form and see the tough times, the years you received no credit because you had no earnings.

As a self-employed person, you pay all of your own Social Security taxes, unlike those who work for others. You pay your personal portion like everyone else, but then you also hand over the matching larger portion that employers pay for employees as part of their taxes. As such, your retirement benefits have taken a hit just because you had the tenacity to stick with it, to cut back and take no pay, to live at or below the poverty line in order to see your business through the bad times.

Two decades later, you've finally built an enterprise that can pay you back for those times that you struggled. But wait! It's time to spread the wealth: new taxes, higher percentages, added costs for each employee, and a general downturn in the economy—all at the same time. There goes your payback—perhaps there go some of your employees, too.

Is this the pursuit of happiness without infringing on another's right to the same? Is this reward or punishment for contributing to society, building a business that provides jobs and wages that are spent back into the economy, thereby making it possible for many to prosper (the multiplier effect)? If this is you, how do you feel about "spread the wealth"?

Help at Last

What if you're a single parent living in poverty with your four children? You have only the most basic skills to offer an employer, and the economy is bad—unemployment is around 10 percent. Someone comes along, say a Presidential candidate, who promises to increase the welfare available to people like you. There will be almost free education so that you can increase your employability, there will be almost free child care while you gain those skills, there will be extended unemployment benefits to carry you for maybe up to two years while you search for a job, and so forth. Do you vote for this person? Of course you do. If this is you, how do you feel about "spread the wealth"?

The Value of Work

Now imagine that you live in a democracy. Perhaps you're an older person who has seen your country go through recessions in the past. You've always worked because you were raised to believe in earning what you receive. Because of this, whenever you've held a job, you've done your very best, putting forth a lot of extra effort for your employers. When others walked, you ran; when they rested, you worked; when they loafed, you persistently did your level best. The result was simple: you never had to go without work. Nothing was beneath you, and excellence was the only thing you took to the job. You did everything with personal pride, as though you were signing off on the task with your promise that you'd done your utmost. Indeed, because of this strong work ethic taught to you by your parents, who had learned it during the Great Depression, you could go to any of your old employers and they'd hire you back in a flash.

So here you are, ready to invest your life savings and start your own business. You begin interviewing candidates and find that they're more interested in what you can give them than in what they can contribute. "How much do you pay? How many paid vacation days? How many sick days? What are the benefits?" That's what you hear from the applicants. Still, you want your dream to come true. Your pursuit of happiness has meant: work hard, save, and eventually start your own business. So you hire the most qualified people. They're the best of the worst, however, and the worst of the best—in short, average.

Your new employees aren't you. They don't hustle. They watch the clock for their breaks and lunch, they arrive 30 seconds before they're required to, and they leave one second after quitting time. They have no loyalty to you or your company and little concern about the new venture's success. Their concern is all about themselves.

You hear of a new minimum wage that will cost you what little reserve you have left. More taxes, higher minimum wages, better health-care packages—more "spread the wealth." How do you like this idea now?

Majority Rules

Remember that in this *What if?* scenario, you live in a democracy—the majority rules. Most people want the wealth spread around because, political candidates claim, the bounty will only be taken from the super rich. You're not one of that upper echelon; you're just an entrepreneur with a new small business and a dream.

The majority would choose to have the wealth spread around—they'd go on the dole if they could still be paid while they were loafing. Most people would prefer entitlement to risk and being average to excellence (especially if there's the possibility they may fail).

It's Election Day. What do you think most people will do? Do you believe that what the majority wants is in the best interest of the country? What if you're the older businessperson in our last scenario. Will you pursue your dream and create jobs, or will you simply retire and enjoy what you have?

Do you believe that the pursuit of happiness is spelled *entitlement?* If not, what about all of those who would work if they could, the people who truly need assistance and aren't exploiting the system? To what degree does the state have an obligation, and when is it overreaching to "spread the wealth"? In other words, how much wealth is it okay to spread?

Whom Do You Want to Help?

What if your neighbors lost their home in a fire? Would you help them with food and shelter? What if a stranger knocked on your door and asked for room and board? What if someone you knew and disapproved of—someone who was lazy and did as little as he could to get by—came to you and asked to be supported? You can see that the answer to the simple question of helping others can get complicated in a hurry. Generally, most people find themselves explaining whom they'd help and under what circumstances. What about you?

Taxes indiscriminately take your money and are used to bribe politicians, pay those who don't want to work for a living, and many similar things. There's a whole potpourri of corrupt distributions of your money with only some of it paying for police, fire, sanitation, education, and other worthwhile purposes. Spreading the wealth is exactly what government does. How much more do you want it to do?

Our society was founded on, and is driven by, entrepreneurial ambitions, freedom, and the pursuit of happiness. How long will it last if it's remodeled to reflect a commune? In a land where the majority rules, isn't it something of a surprise that the country hasn't already been remade as an idyllic dream? Or is it that utopia doesn't work in the real world?

What if you were the one in power—what would you do? What if you were the voter? Would you vote for a redistribution of wealth? What are your ambitions for yourself and for generations to come? What if you could be a deciding factor in the future of your country —would you? Would you get involved?

chapter 15

The Drive for Power

"Religions, which condemn the pleasures of sense, drive men to seek the pleasures of power. Throughout history power has been the vice of the ascetic."

— BERTRAND RUSSELL

What is power? For most people, it's subjective—both good and bad, depending on who wields it, for what purposes, and according to whose definition.

The animal world lives by a hierarchy of power. If the lion goes down to the stream to drink, the antelope hide in the undergrowth nearby to wait their turn. Power also emerges in the play of all children; there are always leaders and followers, and often bullies and the bullied. Even if the mistreatment is limited to words, it's nevertheless bullying. It's the power of will that succeeds when others quit, and it's the lust for power that both builds and destroys kingdoms.

Integrity

For most people, power is something that someone else has—or is it? How do you wield your might? Imagine in this thought experiment that you're the owner of a very posh restaurant, and you've accepted more reservations than you can accommodate. At the busiest point in the evening, with several people agitated and waiting for their table, a party without reservations arrives. It's a large group headed by a very famous person, who wants to be seated now. What do you do?

What if, among this group, is a famous gourmet critic, whom you'd love to have review your restaurant? Add into this situation your reputation for fairness. Indeed, your employees, children, fellow church members, neighbors, and community at large all know you to be an upstanding, honest, and just person. What do you do? Do you seat the party without reservations or turn them away? What if you know that refusing them will lead to an unfavorable article in the newspaper and eventually damage your business enough so that you'll have to lay off several of your employees? At what point do you compromise your integrity—or do you?

Never to Lie

There's an old philosophical quandary that goes like this: Imagine you've promised never to lie or knowingly hurt someone. A married couple, close and dear relatives of yours, are in an automobile accident, and the husband is killed. The wife is in critical condition, and as her next of kin, you're admitted to see her. You're instructed by the physician not to tell her about her husband because the shock could kill her—and the first thing she does is ask you about her husband. Which promise will you break? Will you lie, or will you tell the truth and perhaps cause her death?

Choices are, by and large, what life is about. When our moral principles come into conflict, it's our duty to sort through them and prioritize them carefully.

What if it were your obligation to pay attention and make decisions about a conflict? Imagine that it's your job to read the paper, get to the bottom of the facts, and interview the news makers, just so someone could make a fair and just decision about the matters in contest. Would you want this position?

Power and Spirituality

Think again about power and how you might use it. Do you assert your desires around family and friends? If you don't, do you hunger for a time when you can? Do you sometimes feel inept and lost? Do you internalize your emotions, or do you become angry and shout them out? No matter what your answer is, you're using power. When one of your children behaves badly, do you discipline him or her? Should you? If so, how?

Power is thought of in negative terms among spiritually minded people. Why is that? Even those who seek to be "among the least of them" or to be the proverbial lamb await the power and wrath of their god to set matters straight with those who failed to serve him properly. The divine is the great equalizer for many individuals.

What if power is all a part of being spiritual? Jesus is credited with refraining from calling down the armies of heaven and halting his arrest, and he's considered to be among the most powerful of all who have ever walked this earth. What if the right use of power is as Gandhi applied it, "right action"? In other words, use power to resist corrupt or unlawful power in a nonviolent way.

Inaction is action, which as John Locke said, amounts to tacit consent.[1] Right action is doing the right thing—but what is that? When is there a higher good to be served by doing something we think of as repulsive under different circumstances? If you could save your family by killing a home intruder, would you? If you could save a neighborhood by killing a dozen individuals, would you do it? If you could save your country by nuking another nation, would you do that?

When individuals squarely face conflicts and deal honestly with them, they discover things about themselves. Who are you if you know not what you would or could do? Who are you when you take responsibility for the farmers and the tiny fish, for the restaurant employees and their job security, for the actions of a nation to preserve the lives of its citizens? In other words, who are you if you must be the one making the decision?

What if you get it wrong? Do you take responsibility for your own choices, or would you prefer to abdicate your power to someone else in order to avoid possible blame? Is this why there's so much corruption in the world—because so many choose to hand over their say-so to a select few (governments and other leaders)? What would happen if everyone took full responsibility for everything in their lives? Would the world become a better place, or would current problems just be replaced by new ones?

What if the right path to your spiritual unfoldment depends upon the extent to which you get involved? *What if?*

❖❖❖

chapter 16

Innocent

*"It is better to risk saving a guilty man
than to condemn an innocent one."*

— **Voltaire**

Imagine that you're a court-appointed public defender and you get a call about representing an accused rapist. You accept the case and travel to the jail where you meet your client. He tells you that he has confessed to kidnapping and raping a young woman. He then tells you all the details: he picked her up on a busy corner in Phoenix and drove her out of town, where he beat and raped her. This victim was not his first.

Your job is to defend this man and see that he receives a fair trial, and you discover that his rights were never explicitly made clear to him. He's found guilty in a lower court; you appeal his case and eventually prevail. The Supreme Court sets his conviction aside in a split decision.

How do you feel? You've won your case and set a precedent in doing so. In the future, all subjects who are arrested will have their rights read to them. This is what actually happened in the now-famous *Miranda v. Arizona* case.

Think about this: What if one of the victims is your daughter? How do you feel now? Eventually Miranda was released, so in our thought experiment, let's imagine the rapist leaves jail and commits another rape. This time he so brutally savages a teenage girl that she spends the rest of her life in a mental institution. If you're the attorney, do you share any guilt for this later crime? If you're the parent of the last victim, how do you feel about the attorney when you learn that the perpetrator was set free because of the attorney's work?

Confession

Now imagine that you're an innocent person arrested for a crime because you were in the area where it was committed, you match a general description, and you drive a green compact car. The arresting officers are convinced that you're guilty, so they rough you up and push you for a confession. One of them intimates that you'll save yourself a horrific beating if you admit you did it. You think about it and decide to confess, knowing that you can recant when it is safer to do so. They haul you to the station, where you're shoved, elbowed, and jabbed. The officers carefully deliver their blows with a specific weapon on certain areas of the body so that little evidence of the beating will occur. They believe they have a right—even a duty—to do this, and there's no such thing as a Miranda warning to stop them. How do you feel now?

Conservation or Jobs

There's a highway in this country that has cut off wildlife from the local water source. Every year, there are multiple accidents as drivers swerve to miss creatures ranging from large turtles to four-legged ones of many varieties. Besides the human expense of property and lives, the animal population in the area is being decimated. There's a suggestion to tunnel under the highway in order to create a safe path to the water. The cost would be more than $50 million. The economy is in a serious recession, and national debt is at an all-time high. You're in a position to decide whether to spend the money or not. You must choose between this proposal and another one whose supporters also urgently want the money for their program.

The competing issue is all about jobs. Concern over deforestation is on the rise around the world. There's a logging district nearby, and the citizens of your state have petitioned to stop this work. No new permits are being issued, and several lumber mills have been forced to close. Local unemployment is in the stratosphere, and the economy has been so blighted that many other businesses have closed. If you do nothing, this once-thriving community of tens of thousands will become a ghost town. The fact is that shutting down the logging industry has damaged the statewide economy. From trucking to building supplies, the outlook gets dimmer as time goes on and nothing is done.

You have the power to direct $50 million to the devastated area for reforestation, alternative-energy development, reclamation, and managed forest usage. The proposal suggests that this would solve both the unemployment problem and larger statewide issues. What do you do?

Priorities

Before you decide, imagine that your mother and father own a small grocery store in the community troubled by the lumber shutdown. They're barely hanging on to their business and have already mortgaged everything, including their home, to save the store. If something doesn't happen, their life's savings, everything they've worked for, is lost—gone! They have no other means of support and no place to go, except to move into your already too-small home. You get to choose . . . so what's your decision?

Let's assume this is either-or—there's no way around it. You must choose one or the other. Which gets your nod and why? The *why* is more important than the question itself. Think about what is behind your answer. What have you prioritized? What is your reasoning?

Did you perhaps choose to fund the logging scenario? Did you do so due to economic considerations? The majority would. The real question is why?

For most people, the dollar is more important than the lives of turtles and other creatures. If our priorities were clear in the first place (that is, money over animals), then why was the logging stopped? If, on the other hand, our priority is nature and its conservation, why wouldn't we want to save the animals dependent on the water we took away from them by building a four-lane highway?

Why We Choose What We Choose

Issues are often complex, and decided upon by various people with differing priorities. Most of us find that the issue with the most power over our vote is the one that directly affects *us*. By role-playing, we see how different we feel when the situation is reversed. Harken back to the fish-and-farmer conflict—as the farmer, you have quite a different perspective from the naturalist who brought the issue before the courts. Does this duality exist in part because we're oriented to win or lose rather than simply doing the right thing?

What *is* the right thing? Often, we simply don't know. Given this, should we attempt to err on the conservative side? If so, what side is that? Save the animals or save the people? Save the environment or save the economy? Save our family or save the turtles? The closer to home the question gets, the more passionate we become and the easier the question is to answer.

Where are the innocent? Who are they? If they exist, are there also parties we should blame? Who's guilty, and of what?

The scenarios in this book are relatively easy compared with many we must deal with. Becoming clear about why we feel a certain way under one set of circumstances and another way under different circumstances is what I want to draw out here. Dissonance, which often operates without our awareness, is what we want to discard. Being clear on why we make choices gets us one step closer to understanding ourselves. Knowing ourselves—somehow finding the real self behind all the plastic of what we pretend to be—is perhaps the most important thing we can do. Unfortunately, it's also often the last undertaking we think of.

What if you discovered dissonant values within yourself—what would you do? Do you have the courage to examine and reconcile them? What if you saw them in a loved one? What about a stranger? Do you have any obligation to point it out? How would you react if some-one pointed it out to you?

chapter 17

Camelot

*"I believe that if I should die, and you were to walk
near my grave, from the very depths of the Earth,
I would hear your footsteps."*

— ATTRIBUTED TO BENITO PEREZ GALDOS

When I think of Camelot, I'm reminded of the marvelous musical starring Richard Harris and Vanessa Redgrave. The story is much more than one of a fair kingdom setting matters right by using might—"not might makes right—but might for right." It's also the story of love: Arthur loves Guenevere and Lancelot, Lancelot and Guenevere have an affair, and this forces Arthur to apply the laws of the kingdom and pursue those he loves in battle.

Empty Nesters

Let's try another thought experiment to clarify your thoughts about love and duty. Imagine that you're married to a wonderful person whom you've grown fonder and fonder of over time. You've been married for more than 20 years, and your spouse is your best friend. You've raised three children, and they're all gone, either married or in college. Recently you've been having some differences of opinion as you adjust to being empty nesters—alone with each other and without some run-fetch-and-carry schedule driven by your children. Additionally, both of you are dealing with significant life changes that are affecting your relationship; but you know it, and you're loyal and faithful to your mate even in the bad times.

Soul Mates

One day you happen to quite innocently meet a friend of a friend. You're instantly convinced you've just met your soul mate. Until this point you hadn't believed in soul mates—but here before you is the person you know is meant to be your lover across all time and eternity, your perfect mate, the throb that makes your heart beat. You're stricken with what seems to be a nearly uncontrollable obsession. You go home and Google this person. You close your eyes at night and see the object of your desire in your mind and in your dreams. You attempt to counter the influence, but this person is in your every thought.

What do you do?

Is it possible to love more than one individual? Can you care at different levels? Can you feel affection for one person—on scale of 1 to 10—at a level of 8 and another person at 10? Can you love two individuals at a level of 10, for that matter?

Assume that your spouse meets the other person as well and takes a liking to him or her. Thus, your soul mate is frequently near you, in your home and going places with you. You look each other in the eye, and without a word, you both recognize the bond across forever. The more you see each other, the more difficult it is to stay true to your mate. Do you tell your spouse and keep the other person at arm's length, or do you let happen whatever will happen?

Under the criteria we think of as unconditional love, if you were the other half of the couple, you want the very best for both your spouse and their soul mate, independent of what you gain. So what if they take up with each other, leaving you behind—will that make all of it easier or more difficult?

Guilt

Going back to our original roles, let's assume you leave your spouse for your soul mate. Will you feel guilt over abandoning your best friend of 20-plus years? Can you be happy under such conditions? What if you tell your spouse that he or she isn't your soul mate? Will that benefit you in any way?

What if you married originally for lukewarm reasons or for purposes other than love of any kind—perhaps for money, power, prestige, or escape—whatever the reason, it wasn't love. Yet for more than two decades, your spouse has been faithful to you, supported you, and cared for you in every way, even doted upon you, knowing that your love was less than his or hers. Would that make it any easier to say good-bye and go with your soul mate? Is it ever appropriate to divorce due to one partner's attraction to another person?

What if knowing who your soul mate was caused you to be bitter about your marriage due to your inability to be with the person you now yearned for with every ounce of your being? Would this justify your leaving your spouse—after all, isn't he or she entitled to more love than you're able to give?

What Is Love?

Much of modern science would have us believe that love is only a chemical reaction. Indeed, according to some, it might even be a chemical addiction between people. In the words of Swiss psychologist Carl Jung: "The meeting of two personalities is like the contact of two chemical substances: if there's any reaction, both are transformed." Of course, Jung was saying this long before modern science demonstrated the chemical reaction and bonding to be a fact.

We must also remember a truth articulated by many people in many ways, and put into these words by author Henry Bromel: "Sometimes when you look back on a situation, you realize it wasn't all you thought it was. A beautiful girl walked into your life. You fell in love. Or did you? Maybe it was only a childish infatuation, or maybe just a brief moment of vanity." So what is love?

Is it possible that it's both chemical and a bridge across forever, as author Richard Bach describes it?

Perhaps the chemistry is a sort of "prewiring" that aids us in finding the right person. But what if you married too soon and for the wrong reasons and then found that special person—what then?

Is loyalty a form of devotion? Is honesty a form of integrity? Is there any virtue in leaving a spouse of 20-plus years? Is there less integrity in denying the passion that exists between you and your soul mate?

What if you had been thinking about feeling lonely or disconnected from your spouse when you met your would-be soul mate? Would it be easier or more difficult to dismiss the thoughts and feelings?

Here's your real *What if?* What if you were one of the married couple's children and it was your parent dealing with this struggle. What would you advise, and why? What if you could look into the hearts of all parties —what would you recommend?

Love moves mountains, it's said. It's also said that this is the strongest force in the universe. Do the proverbs mean caring for another above oneself, or is it passion —how that person makes you feel?

I submit that what conquers all is the love that knows the bond of loyalty, the honor of integrity, the compassion of true friendship, and the unconditional devotion that puts the needs of another above oneself.

What if this is true? What if it's false? What does it mean to you?

chapter 18

Human Rights

*"The twentieth century has been characterized
by three developments of great political importance:
the growth of democracy, the growth of corporate power,
and the growth of corporate propaganda as a means
of protecting corporate power against democracy."*

— ALEX CAREY

What if the nations of the world agreed to a standard of human rights? Would they—could they—enforce such a standard? Could there be a universal rule of law that brings peace to our world?

After the atrocities of World War II, the nations of the world did gather, and nearly every major country eventually signed on to a charter designed to put a protective umbrella over all human beings. Those agreeing to this protective charter included Afghanistan, Argentina, Australia, Belgium, Bolivia, Brazil, Burma, Canada, Chile, China, Colombia, Costa Rica, Cuba, Denmark, the Dominican Republic, Ecuador, Egypt, El Salvador, Ethiopia, France, Greece, Guatemala, Haiti, Iceland,

India, Iran, Iraq, Lebanon, Liberia, Luxembourg, Mexico, Netherlands, New Zealand, Nicaragua, Norway, Pakistan, Panama, Paraguay, Peru, Philippines, Thailand, Sweden, Syria, Turkey, United Kingdom, United States, Uruguay, and Venezuela. The Soviet bloc countries abstained from the vote.

Failure to Act

World War II taught everyone not to turn a blind eye to actions against the innocent, no matter who the perpetrator might be. Further, it was recognized that the failure of countries and individuals to act against the persecution of others might have actually fanned the flames of war that eventually engulfed the entire world. The United Nations General Assembly Resolution 217 A (III) was therefore adopted, and proclaimed the Universal Declaration of Human Rights on December 10, 1948. Afterward, the assembly called upon all its member countries "to cause it to be disseminated, displayed, read and expounded principally in schools and other educational institutions, without distinction based on the political status of countries or territories."[1]

What are these rights proclaimed in the document? The preamble sets out the basic purpose of the declaration:

> Whereas recognition of the inherent dignity and of the equal and inalienable rights of all members of the human family is the foundation of freedom, justice and peace in the world,
> Whereas disregard and contempt for human rights have resulted in barbarous acts, which have outraged

the conscience of mankind, and the advent of a world in which human beings shall enjoy freedom of speech and belief, and freedom from fear and want has been proclaimed as the highest aspiration of the common people,

Whereas it is essential, if man is not to be compelled to have recourse, as a last resort, to rebellion against tyranny and oppression, that human rights should be protected by the rule of law,

Whereas it is essential to promote the development of friendly relations between nations,

Whereas the peoples of the United Nations have in the Charter reaffirmed their faith in fundamental human rights, in the dignity and worth of the human person and in the equal rights of men and women, and have determined to promote social progress and better standards of life in larger freedom,

Whereas Member States have pledged themselves to achieve, in co-operation with the United Nations, the promotion of universal respect for and observance of human rights and fundamental freedoms,

Whereas a common understanding of these rights and freedoms is of the greatest importance for the full realization of this pledge,

Now, Therefore THE GENERAL ASSEMBLY proclaims THIS UNIVERSAL DECLARATION OF HUMAN RIGHTS as a common standard of achievement for all peoples and all nations, to the end that every individual and every organ of society, keeping this Declaration constantly in mind, shall strive by teaching and education to promote respect for these rights and freedoms and by progressive measures, national and international, to secure their universal and effective recognition and observance, both among the peoples of Member States themselves and among the peoples of territories under their jurisdiction.[2]

The articles delineate the declaration of rights, and I've included them in their entirety in the Appendix. This is a fascinating document, and there are some articles in particular that are worth examining further. But first, did you know that the Universal Declaration of Human Rights and its articles even existed? Are you surprised to learn that most Americans have no idea it does?

Whom Do You Care For?

What if you picked up the Sunday paper and read about an earthquake in Haiti? Tens of thousands are thought to be dead; the country is in ruins. Do you open up your pocketbook and make a donation? Probably. Do you recognize suffering from the stories told in the news? Again, probably. Is there sympathy in your heart for those who survived? Do you feel connected to those who are in trouble? That's the spirit of brotherhood.

Now imagine that you open the paper and read about your archenemy—we'll say Osama bin Laden. His encampment was just struck by a huge earthquake, and the surrounding area is in ruins. It looks as if most people there are dead. Do you have the same feeling of empathy now? Or does enmity overwhelm brotherhood and give rise to celebrating, as many did in the Middle East when the Twin Towers in New York were leveled by terrorists?

The Bible quotes Jesus as warning that whatever we do unto the least of our brothers we do unto him. I watched a recent TV news broadcast that showed a Muslim man in his early 20s, living in the UK, telling the reporter he wasn't Christian—so of course he wouldn't turn the other cheek! No, he would exact revenge. The interviewer had simply asked if the young man thought the violence against the Western world was justified. Not only did he think it was justified, but the young Islamist relished the idea that unlike those who might insist on turning the other cheek, he wouldn't just get even—he'd get "evener"!

Genocide

Article 2 of the UN document states that everyone is entitled to the rights set out in the declaration, regardless of any number of factors, including the nature of the government they live under. According to the declaration, then, there's no reason for a signatory state to hesitate for a minute when it learns of genocide somewhere in the world. Yet there's hesitation, negotiation, and even turning a blind eye to such reports while innocents are raped, tortured, and killed.

What if you believe that America isn't the world's police force, so you oppose sending American troops to other nations? Do you also oppose humanitarian aid, as with the earthquake in Haiti? Probably not. Are you against sending troops to Darfur to end the genocide there? Some might be. How do you feel about toppling a genocidal government, such as that in Serbia during the ethnic cleansing of the 1990s? What are your feelings about bringing down a despot who paid thousands of dollars to families in Palestine who sent relatives into Israel with suicide bombs to kill and terrorize Israelis? What if you oppose the war in Iraq, and then find out that the person paying bounties to families of suicide bombers was none other than Saddam Hussein?

Perhaps you read the articles of the UN declaration and thought how nice it would be if they were followed. Maybe as you filter out the possibilities, disambiguate some of the ramifications, and so forth, you feel differently. American attorney Michael Newdow points out:

> People don't simply wake up one day and commit genocide. They start by setting themselves apart from others, diminishing the stature of those adhering to dissenting beliefs in small, insidious steps. They begin by saying, "We're the righteous, and we'll tolerate those others," and as the toleration diminishes over time, the inevitable harms are overlooked. It is for that reason that James Madison wisely wrote that "it is proper to take alarm at the first experiment on our liberties."[3]

What do you tolerate? What do you feel righteous about? Was President George W. Bush right to go after Saddam Hussein, even if there were no weapons of mass destruction, for at worst, he was only enforcing Article 2 of the UN declaration?

"Collateral damage" is what the military calls the loss of innocent lives during war. What would you call the acts of Saddam Hussein? Should he have been removed, according to Article 2? When do you choose to enforce the rules and when not? French biologist and philosopher Jean Rostand may add some clarity to this issue, at least from the perspective of history, with this comment: "Kill a man, and you are an assassin. Kill millions of men, and you are a conqueror. Kill everyone, and you are a god."[4]

Capital Punishment

Article 3 of the UN declaration says that everyone has a right to life, liberty, and security of person. What if you wake up one morning, turn on the morning news while sipping your first cup of coffee, and hear that a man has come forward and admitted to killing a woman in a locally famous case. You know the details of the murder because you were on the jury that convicted the wrong man. You remember how he protested his innocence throughout the trial. A sudden thump hits your gut—you were a party to taking the life of an innocent man.

There was a moratorium on capital punishment during the 1970s while the interpretation of the Eighth Amendment phrase "cruel and unusual punishment" was litigated. The Supreme Court reinstated the death penalty in 1976. During the moratorium, capital-crime rates fell. For 2007, the average murder rate in states with the death penalty was 5.5 per 100,000 people; the average for the 14 states without the death penalty was 3.1. From the reinstatement through December 2008, there were 1,136 executions in the United States. In 2004, four nations (China, Iran, Vietnam, and the United States) accounted for 97 percent of all global executions. On average, every nine to ten days a state government in the United States executes a prisoner.[5]

European nations oppose the death penalty. Should they take steps under Article 3 to halt its use? What if someone you loved was brutally murdered? Would you want the killer to pay with his or her life? What if you learned that by the time a capital prisoner exhausted his or her legal remedies, it cost more to execute the prisoner than to incarcerate him for life—would you still favor execution? (When you consider the costs of a capital-crime trial, together with all of the appeals and the nearly unlimited resources provided by the state to ensure that the criminal has every defense under the law, you discover that it does indeed cost more than a life sentence.) What if your child were on trial in a country such as North Korea for crossing the border by mistake? What if the sentence was capital punishment? Would you have more hope if the verdict were life in prison?

Taxes

Article 4 prohibits slavery in all forms. Robert Nozick, a famed philosopher and Harvard professor, believed that taxes are an instrument of slavery. What if the taxes are unjust—unequal? What if some pay nothing while others pay 45 percent or more of their income—is that fair? Are those who make money the slaves of the system that takes their earnings for redistribution via big government? Or is this the fairest way to preserve the opportunity to make big bucks in the first place? Are there other options or a sliding scale to this calculation?

It has long been noted that if someone comes to your home to occupy it by force or to steal its contents, you'll resist. If, however, that someone represents the banker repossessing your home due to failure to repay the mortgage, then you lower your head in shame and walk away. Is debt not a form of indentured servitude?

It's popular today to sling slogans such as: "You're not free if health care is not free." Tomorrow it may be popular to use the motto: "You're not free if your home is not free." (Perhaps by the time this book is published, it already will be!) Is either of these statements true? Is it a human right to have a home and health care?

Torture and Cruel and Unusual Punishment

Article 5 covers torture and cruel and unusual punishment. Under this article, water boarding may be considered a violation. What if you need to obtain information that could save thousands of lives, and you've used all normal means available in your interrogation of an enemy combatant but failed to get anything. You know the data is in this person's head, between his ears. You refuse to pull fingernails or do any permanent physical harm; but you know that using bright lights, sleep deprivation, loud noises, water boarding, and even humiliation could get you what you need. You've successfully used water boarding on others. Do you compromise your principles to save a few thousand lives, or do you pass on the alternative techniques? Do you rationalize that these methods do no permanent physical harm and therefore aren't torture? Would you use water boarding if your loved ones were among those who would die without the needed information?

Have you ever explained away a behavior? Perhaps you've punished one of your children harshly because he or she did something you deemed unusually harmful. Perhaps you've lied to your significant other to protect him or her from being hurt.

Enemy Combatants

Articles 6 through 10 deal generally with equal protection under the law. Some would argue that these
provisions mean trying so-called enemy combatants in
American courts instead of before military tribunals.
The traditional way has always been to try combatants under military law, but the Obama administration
would like to move more and more such individuals
into U.S. courtrooms. There they would receive their
Miranda warnings and clam up. They could use the
rights and privileges of American citizens to put their
cases on trial, to tell their stories, and to work the system. If the system is as just and fair as we believe it to
be, perhaps they could be set free on some technicality.
Remember my description of how the Miranda warning became part of U.S. police practice? Ernesto Miranda
himself was set free after confessing to the brutal rape
of a young woman. The truth is, Miranda committed
the crime, but because the court ruled that the confession was unlawfully gained (he was beaten before he
confessed), the information was thrown out of court.
Voilà—the Miranda warning came into being (you have
the right to remain silent, anything you say can and
will be used against you in a court of law, and so forth).

What if you lost a loved one in the attacks of 9/11
and the accused mastermind, Khalid Sheikh Mohammed, is moved to trial in New York—in your backyard,
in the very city where the atrocity took place. Not far
from where your loved one died, this man, intent on
doing harm to as many Americans as possible, would
receive a fair trial, despite having already admitted his
guilt. His confession, however, may be in question, just

as Miranda's was. (At the time of this writing, and due to all the protests, it looks highly improbable that the trial will be held in a civilian court at all—but what if it had been?)

Innocent Until Proven Guilty

Article 11 presumes innocence. The current administration, under President Barack Obama, assures us that Khalid Sheikh Mohammed won't go free, no matter what. Then why try him? Is this equal protection under the law, or is there some hidden agenda? If we try him, doesn't our system require the presumption of innocence, or is there something else at work here? Is this a new form of segregation or special profiling? Is it the spirit or the letter of the law that's being followed when someone presumed guilty is nevertheless given a trial in an American court by his "peers"?

Right to Privacy

Article 12 guarantees the right to privacy. Governments of the world are intent on defending their citizens against terrorists today. In the name of protection, in the name of security—national safety—the privacy rights of law-abiding individuals are being trampled. Should they be?

Imagine that electronic eavesdropping uncovers a plot to release a dirty bomb in the heavily populated city where you and your loved ones live. The would-be perpetrators are arrested and the weapon is disposed of safely. Are you grateful for the eavesdropping, even if you later find out that when you used Google to figure out how to spell Zacarias Moussaoui's name, your search was tracked and recorded by the U.S. government's intelligence people?

Thought Police

Where is the trade-off between safety and freedom? Anyone who has read George Orwell's *1984* knows how easy it is to lose all of one's rights. The thought police can be on every corner, yet no one wishes to return to the era of Senator Joseph McCarthy and the "Red Scare"—or do they?

Marriage

It's easy to see that there are potential conflicts for every article in the UN declaration. Resolution requires an unbiased arbitrator, and some may simply be irresolvable. Rather than continue through them one by one, let's discuss only a few more that highlight contemporary issues. Article 16, for example, states that marriage is between a man and a woman. This is a major issue of contention in the United States at the time of this writing. Does that mean U.S. sovereignty should be turned over to a world court and this dispute handled there?

Social Insurance

Article 22 is about social security, which is defined as "primarily a social insurance program providing social protection, or protection against socially recognized conditions, including poverty, old age, disability, unemployment, and others."[6] Perhaps it isn't far-fetched to think that sometime in the future, people will have a right to free housing and no longer be vulnerable to encumbrances that, as with the housing bubble and subprime-loan crisis of the first decade of the 21st century, lead to foreclosures that rip up lives.

What if you learned that the idea behind the subprime-loan debacle was to make the great American dream of home ownership possible? Lending institutions were forced by the government to meet quotas that included loans that, with 20/20 hindsight, simply shouldn't have been made. Indeed, the only hope there ever was for repayment of most of them was in the housing bubble itself. In other words, real-estate prices had to continue to increase so that the homes with subprime loans could be sold for higher amounts, thereby removing real equity. Most lenders believed they wouldn't be at risk, because housing was increasing along with demand, and if loans failed, they could simply resell the properties for more than was owed. If you learned that home ownership was the idea behind the subprime loans and, according to Article 22, something everyone is entitled to, would you be upset if you lost your house?

What if messing with the economy in this way led to financial failures and wiped out long-standing financial institutions? What if, to add fuel to the fire, you had investments in these institutions that were for your retirement—and now they've simply evaporated? Yesterday you were ready to retire, and today you're looking at having to work well into your 70s. How do you feel about Article 22 now? What if it were your child's college fund that disappeared in an instant because of some well-meaning bureaucrat? What if your savings were in the stock of a failed institution? Now they're gone. What if you'd planned to withdraw the money to cover the expense of a life-saving operation needed by a loved one? No money—no operation.

Obviously do-good ideas can do great harm.

Lifestyle

Articles 23 through 25 deal with lifestyle, asserting that everyone has a right to one that includes time for leisure. Further, everyone is entitled to a job and/ or unemployment insurance. Notice that there are no provisions for how well individuals must work or how much they should contribute to their employer, but there's an assurance that they can organize in unions for collective bargaining. Where in the Constitution of the United States are these rights guaranteed? Consider the rights guaranteed under the Constitution and those set forth in the Universal Declaration of Human Rights. What if there's a conflict between the two documents? Which one do you think should prevail?

Human rights imply, at least to me, certain responsibilities. Where the ideas of the UN declaration are well meaning and might work in a perfect world, how are we either to get to that perfect world or to resolve the differences that arise out of this document?

It's incumbent upon each of us to participate in the process that determines the future for everyone. What if it were all up to you? What would you do? What rules or rights, if any, would you change? What would you add? Why? What if you were wrong?

chapter 19

E Followed by *F*

*"What we want is to see the child in pursuit of knowledge,
and not knowledge in pursuit of the child."*

— GEORGE BERNARD SHAW

Consider this statement by educator and "hierarchiologist" Laurence Peter: "Education is a method whereby one acquires a higher grade of prejudices." What if that's true? Who's creating the script that contains the prejudice, and for what purpose? I've said in earlier writings: "Control the definition and you control the argument." Is that true?

What if you're 17 years old, in your last semester of high school with less than two months until graduation, living on your own and working a job to support yourself, when you're called into the principal's office. You know the reason for the summons can't be your grades, because you have straight *A*'s. You're expecting to be valedictorian of the school because you have a perfect 4.0 GPA. You're an emancipated youth, and as such, you're paying your bills and acing your classes—so why does the principal want to see you?

Imagine you enter his office and are told that you won't graduate with the rest of your class. It seems you've missed too many days. The principal, whom you've never liked and who seems to feel the same way about you, informs you that the school is paid a dollar per day for your attendance; when you miss school, they don't get their money, and that means you don't graduate. You'll have to go to summer school so that the institution receives the money it needs before you can graduate. What do you do? Do you go to summer school, or do you quit and take the pay raise and full-time position offered by your employer? Do you get a GED, or do you just bag it? Whatever you decide to do, what's your opinion of this kind of situation?

This actually happened to me, and I chose to walk away. Later, I matriculated at Weber State University, my undergraduate alma mater, where I tested out of a year's worth of college credit by using the College Level Examination Program (CLEP) tests. No GED, no high school diploma, one year of college credit on the basis of examination, and I was off again—studying because I chose to learn. I'd been told there was a graduate scholarship waiting for me in political science if I wanted it, but since I didn't graduate from high school, I had to pay for my own college education. It's too bad that my high school hadn't let me pay the dollar a day for the missed time—it would probably have cost me 60 bucks or less.

What Are We Being Taught . . . and Why?

When we go to school, we expect to be educated. We don't even remotely suspect that the education is a fraud. *E* stands for education, and *F* doesn't mean flunking but outright fraud. That's a pretty bold statement, so let's see if it's also fair.

When I went to school, and I'll bet the same is true for you, I was taught falsehoods. For example, I was taught that Thomas Edison invented the lightbulb. The fact is, the lightbulb was invented by Joseph Swan. It seems that Edward Bernays, the founder of modern marketing and the author of the book *Propaganda,* put together a marketing extravaganza in 1929 called Light's Golden Jubilee. This history-changing event gave credit to Edison for the invention, and the marketing hype has burned itself into textbooks everywhere.[1] You were probably also taught that at the time of Columbus, people believed the earth to be flat. That's also totally false. The reason for that widespread falsehood, however, is even more interesting than the false belief about the inventor of the lightbulb.

Science and Religion

In 1876, Andrew Dickson White, the first president of Cornell University—the first university not to have a religious affiliation—wrote the now-infamous *Warfare of Science.*[2] In 1896 he turned this so-called text into a more ponderous two-volume work entitled *A History of the Warfare of Science with Theology in Christendom.*[3] According to White, there was a great, long-standing rift between science and religion, a point simply not supported by fact. Indeed, even a quick look in that direction reveals that at the time, there was little separation between the two in the minds of those we call scientists. For them, the natural world revealed the workings of God. It didn't occur to most scientists before 1800 that science challenged God. The idea of conflict was promulgated by two men, Andrew Dickson White and John William Draper, who wrote *History of the Conflict between Religion and Science* in 1874.[4] Draper was a passionate English Methodist minister whose work openly assailed Catholicism. White, it's believed, "was provoked by criticism he received for establishing Cornell without religious affiliation."[5] The fact is that both texts are embarrassments to true historians. Indeed, Professor Lawrence Principe of Johns Hopkins University flatly states that the books belong in a museum of how not to do history.[6]

Who Believed the World Was Flat?

It was White who decided to provide the notion of the flat world in connection with Columbus.[7] You can shake your finger at your teacher, or perhaps your child's teacher, on this one, for they had to know this information was wrong. They knew it but failed to recognize that they did. Why do I say that? The same teachers who tell stories about Columbus also tell us that 300 years before Christ, Greek astronomer Eratosthenes calculated the earth's circumference to be 24,700 miles. Today, we know it to be 24,902 miles. Let me say that again: 300 years before Christ, Greeks were aware that the earth was round and knew its size within approximately one percent of its actual circumference, and this is a well-known fact. This knowledge was never lost. In Columbus's time, the argument was that ships weren't large enough to carry enough supplies. The belief that the earth was flat was simply made up by Andrew Dickson White.[8]

Twisting History

I could go on to point out more factual errors in schoolbooks, but my point is this: Who checks on those who write the textbooks that provide the basis for opinions we all hold? Have you checked any of them? Do you know how many private agendas are served by twisting history? Do you know how many factual errors are likely to occur in the most heavily checked texts? Try it. According to Mel Gabler's Educational Research Analysts:

> In 2002, for the first time in 11 years, publishers submitted high school U.S. history books for Texas approval . . . and again the education establishment missed most factual errors. In 1991, we found 231 undetected factual errors in six high school U.S. history books after the state approval process certified them error-free. When this year's process ended, we found 249 still-uncorrected factual errors in four books— more mistakes overlooked in fewer texts. This despite publishers' claims to have beefed up their fact-checking, despite Texas Education Agency emphasis on verifying accuracy to the State Textbook Review Panel, and despite an $80,000 Texas Tech review team backing them up.

No one claims we call ideological differences "factual errors." These 249 errors were all the "2+2=5" type of mistakes that both Jesse Jackson and Jesse Helms would agree are wrong. From publishers' lists of editorial changes, it is plain that they often use mostly proofreaders, not real academicians, to troubleshoot. Of course they market textbooks on the basis of teaching aids, not subject matter content. The Texas Education Commissioner's Report on Correction of Factual Errors combined the findings of the State Textbook Review Panel and the findings of the $80,000 Texas Tech textbook review team. In all the high school U.S. history books, this report recommended a grand total of four changes. Pitiful.

Almost certainly the respective eighth-grade companion volumes of these four high school U.S. history books contain a like number of undiscovered factual errors. In the more than 100 total texts in this K-12 Social Studies submission, the factual errors yet outstanding must run into the thousands. What if this industry flew our airplanes or made our prescription drugs?[9]

Today, this information is even more interesting because of the recent coverage of the Texas School Board and the influence they have over the content of textbooks used by schools throughout the U.S.[10]

Textual Errors

What are some of these textual errors—information that you may think is factual? Well, just so you get a flavor of the kind of mistakes present in so-called history textbooks, here are a handful of examples:

- Columbus never reached North America. He explored the Caribbean islands and the northern coast of South America.

- U.S. development of the atomic bomb was no secret to Stalin. The Venona cables show he knew of it by 1941 and that Soviet spies kept close watch on it thereafter.

- The U.S. did not gain Texas as result of the Mexican-American War. Texas was annexed in 1845, before that war began.

- The British did not surrender after the Battle of New Orleans. They withdrew.[11]

These examples are all the truth, but this is not what was published in the approved textbooks.

Imagine 249 such errors just in American history. What of the other textbooks purporting to give us facts about world history, political science, and so forth? You'll quickly discover that there are many books about the errors in the texts you commit to memory, if just for examination day. The titles of some of these works are telling—for example, *Some Lies and Errors of History.*[12]

Agendas

In the book *48 Liberal Lies About American History,* we see illustrated the meaning of the word *agenda.* In this work by Larry Schweikart, a history professor at the University of Dayton, we see the workings of a political point of view—a lens, if you will—interpreting historical events as if he were a modern television pundit spinning his political interest on the Sunday-morning television talk shows.[13] And I do mean spin.

In early 2010, three different spokespeople for President Obama were out on the Sunday-morning circuit heralding the success of the stimulus money. Valerie Jarrett claimed it saved "thousands and thousands of jobs." Press Secretary Robert Gibbs claimed it saved "1.5 million jobs." David Axelrod stated on CNN's *State of the Union:* "But understand that, in this recession that began at the beginning of 2007, we've lost 7 million jobs. Now, the Recovery Act the President passed has created more than—or saved more than 2 million jobs. But against 7 million, you know, that—that is—it is cold comfort to those who still are looking."[14]

Politically Correct

What's the truth? According to Schweikart, over the past 40 years, history books have become more, shall we say, politically correct. The result, he argues, is that high school and even college graduates enter society with distorted ideas and beliefs about foreign policy, economics, religion, war, race relations, and more. If you discover that what you thought was true is false—what will you do? How will you amend the error? Is it necessary to go back to school to relearn or unlearn everything you've been taught that's false? Is there a class somewhere called "Unlearning the Erroneous Facts" so that you can be set free from their influence? Should there be?

How many times have you decided an issue based on what you thought was true? How many times have you taken sides, especially in politics, based on totally fictitious presuppositions; implicit assumptions; and beliefs formed from the information in supposedly authoritative textbooks? How many times have you accepted the word of your teachers without checking where they got their facts? If you admit that your insight could be flawed because your learning is in error—then what do you do? What if you had the power to correct all this—what would you do?

Reassessing the Data

We think in certain ways and use specific tools to come to our decisions. Whenever we engage the thinking/decision/problem-solving system or mental process, we may: rely on memories, seek to identify patterns, calculate in a deductive fashion, use inductive processes, extrapolate from learned generalizations, be influenced by our own hidden biases and implicit assumptions, and more. We may even decide to attempt some experimentation, such as taking our own survey or adding a gallon of water to a gallon of alcohol to see if the result is more or less than two gallons. We'll definitely draw upon our experience and perhaps argue vociferously that we know Columbus discovered America because we remember the day our teacher showed us a film about his voyage. Perhaps we'll design a model, as does a friend of mine who builds mock-ups for everything from relationships to chemistry. Once the model is in hand, maybe we'll begin to add attributes or different characteristics, build up metaphors, generate examples, deduce a hypothesis, or in less-systematic ways set about settling on our own opinion of the *facts*.

Mind Programming

The problem is obvious: What if all the underlying information from which we build our models, our explanations, and so forth is wrong, and we don't know it? What then? Maybe we only think we know about some things. Perhaps we're as wrong about what we think we know of ourselves as we might be about all those other errors. When an argument proceeds from a statement thought to be true, but which is actually false, the argument isn't likely to reach a faithful conclusion. By "faithful," I mean the same answer we'd get if we knew all the undistorted facts.

For example, if you believe that the only reason President Abraham Lincoln sought to free the slaves was so he could add their ranks to the armed forces fighting the South, your opinion of Lincoln isn't the only thing affected. The cause of the Civil War is called into question. If the statements I've just made are true, what justified the war? If you continue with this line of thinking, you begin to ask other questions, such as, *Why did Lincoln suspend habeas corpus?*

As you can see, everything changes when the underlying *facts* change. What, then, are sane and rational people supposed to do when they discover so many falsehoods, so much propaganda, and so few unbiased sources in presumably authoritative textbooks and other supposedly reliable sources of information? Add to this—as I've explained in great detail in my book *Mind Programming*—that the intentional manipulation of facts happens not just through so-called pundits and video news releases (VNRs, as they're popularly called, which almost certainly should be thought of as infomercials).

It also takes place using the most sophisticated techno-
logical means and employing every psychological com-
pliance principle known to humankind. There's little
chance that the average person will even have a clue
about what's really going on.[15]

A Different You

What if you could inform everyone you knew of
this? Would you? Would you dare to break with con-
vention and address the matter from an informed basis?
What if you decided to take the time to really analyze
everything you believe? Would you come away with
some new beliefs, even perhaps a different you?

British psychiatrist Ronald D. Laing asserts a mean-
ingful message in his book *The Politics of Experience:*

> The condition of alienation, of being asleep, of being
> unconscious, of being out of one's mind, is the condition
> of the normal man.
>
> Society highly values its normal man. It educates
> children to lose themselves and to become absurd, and
> thus to be normal.
>
> Normal men have killed perhaps 100,000,000 of
> their fellow men in the past fifty years.
>
> We are not able even to think adequately about
> the behavior that is at the annihilating edge. But what
> we think is less than what we know; what we know is
> less than what we love; what we love is so much less
> than what there is. And to this precise extent we are so
> much less than what we are.[16]

Around the turn of the 20th century, the French
writer Anatole France summed it all up this way: "An

education isn't how much you have committed to memory, or even how much you know. It's being able to differentiate between what you do know and what you don't." What is there that you don't know? What if you learned that much of what you believe was simply an idea framed in an appealing context but with no real substance? What if you discovered that the very foundations upon which you based your beliefs were actually fake? What then?

chapter 20

Certainty

"Although our intellect always longs for clarity and certainty, our nature often finds uncertainty fascinating."

— CARL VON CLAUSEWITZ

What is certain? As we've pondered before, is there anything at all we can say that we know for sure? I suppose we can turn to the world of logic and assert that we know analytic statements to be true. An analytic statement is essentially a definition, such as: "A bachelor is an unmarried man." Sometimes referred to as tautologies because they're circular, they actually tell us nothing. As such, the only thing certain about them is the hope of agreement with respect to the definition. For example, if we created a sentence that's agreed upon today, we'd find that the definition could change in the future and thereby invalidate the analytic statement. Take the word *marriage* and its current meaning in many documents— "between a man and a woman"—and we see how this might happen.

A Priori Knowledge

We could argue that some knowledge is built into the human system and is apprehended *a priori* (known without need for analysis). For example, there's no number too large that one can't be added to it. This seems to be a statement that's internally consistent, so there's no need to teach it. We seem to be made in such a way that logic is a reflection of how we think, so when the argument follows the method consistently, we nod our heads in agreement, saying to ourselves, *That makes sense.*

We can see that there are some matters we can be reasonably sure of, even though this is admittedly a very shallow and extremely brief introduction to the idea of *certainty,* an area of inquiry well worth examining but beyond the scope of this work. How about real life? What can we be definite about there? How does real life differ from the logic of "no number too large for one to be added to it"?

Dealing with Carnage

Shortly after the earthquake in Haiti in January 2010, I was watching television while walking on my treadmill. The news was all about the events in Port-au-Prince, and the footage was of absolute devastation. The scenes cut back and forth between rubble and bodies; some of the bodies were covered, like that of an infant perhaps two or three months old whose bare feet stuck out from under a blanket. The carnage was so upsetting that I couldn't watch the footage. I switched the channel and found the game show *Deal or No Deal,* where college contestants were playing for $500,000. It was frolic and fun, laughter and sighs. In the end, one player walked away richer by $28,000. Both of these events were going on in my recreation room, separated only by the click of my remote control.

Life does go on, as it must. I could imagine the anchorman delivering the news and then leaving the studio after the broadcast to go for drinks with his friends and co-workers. Does that seem right—that so much suffering could be so close, yet so many can and do just go on, seemingly impervious to it all?

What if you were in charge of the news? Would you allow graphic footage to be aired? Do you think such images desensitize people, making it easier for them to compartmentalize the dramas?

How about all the violence and gore in the world of entertainment? Is it possible that we become so accustomed to images of this kind that when we see *real* scenes, we just switch off from them, too?

Life doesn't come with a guarantee. Today may be your last day—there's no certainty that you'll be here for even another hour. You're reminded of this truth almost continually in today's 24/7 news cycle. What if you had nothing to give and nothing you could do to help? What would be left?

Poor Souls

Poverty isn't a natural state of the soul. A poor soul has been made that way by its owner; rich ones are those who are aware of life, death, and the journey, which holds many levels of learning within it. Rich souls always have something they can do, such as pray.

Prayer is a powerful healing agent, a truth that data has now repeatedly demonstrated, including in double-blind studies.[1] What if you knew that your prayers made a difference to others—would you pray?

One thing is for sure: we can be certain that our concern for others will prompt us to remember the fragility of life and to do all we can to support those in need. The problem, as we've seen, can be in defining those in need. What if you wrote the definitions—could you state them in a finite, concrete way? What if knowing yourself depended upon your definitions, for they're the reflection of who and what you believe? Are you other than what you believe? If so, what? What if I truly knew myself at all levels of my being? Would I know what I believe?

chapter 21

Biases?

"Easy is an adjective used to describe a woman
who has the sexual morals of a man."

— Nancy Linn Desmond

Think about bias in our society. In her fascinating book *An Inconvenient Lie: Secrets in Language*, Louise Gouëffic shows how language is often used as a tool to control the masses, to motivate support for wars, to identify enemies, to perpetrate genocide, and more.[1] The bottom line, as I explain in detail in my book *Mind Programming*, is that whoever controls the definitions, controls the argument.[2]

Gouëffic observes that language often "embeds lies, secrets, contradictions, false theory and irrationality in symbols." Continuing, she argues that "words and names assume one half of the species to be dominant as if this is 'the way it is,' as if this is the way the species was 'created.' This 4000-year-old lie is believed as 'Truth.' Patriarchal language is the only language we have, know and use. Lies make confusion, which leads to failure."[3]

In a nutshell, Gouëffic's argument is that women are subservient and continue to be, despite modern efforts in some countries to end this nonsensical belief. Reinforcing their position is a language that fails to treat all equally, has built-in biases, and differentiates on the basis of humor or the basis of political maneuvering.[4] Definitions do control!

The Dictionary

Take, for example, the rollout of the 2009 Homeland Security Domestic Extremism Lexicon. This government publication came on the heels of the election of President Barack Obama. The dictionary is sent to law-enforcement agencies and becomes a kind of watch-list for terrorists or potential terrorists. There was an outcry by many conservatives over this document, because among the so-called extremists were groups and organizations such as Right to Life (opposition to abortion), Second Amendment supporters (gun rights), and returning veterans from Iraq and Afghanistan. Well, the identification of veterans caught everyone's attention, and Janet Napolitano quickly recalled the publication, apologizing and stating a mistake had been made.[5] Was this an accident?

Think back to your days in history class. If you're old enough, you'll remember learning about those Native American *savages*. Cast as barbarians, renegades, and the like, American history showed us the largest genocide yet recorded. Indeed, in his book *American Holocaust*, scholar David Stannard documents the greatest acts of genocide the world has ever experienced: "In 1492, some 100 million native people lived in the Americas. By the end of the 19th century almost all of them had been exterminated. Many died as a result of disease, but the mass extinction was also engineered."[6]

If you wish to marginalize someone, whether a group or an individual, there are two immediate and proven ways to do that. Laugh at them—get everyone to laugh at them—or define them in the most unattractive of ways. Doing both is even better.

Breaking Through Definitions

Take this example: Sarah Palin was a successful and popular governor in her home state of Alaska. She had taken on the old-boy networks of big oil and big business and beaten them at their own game, returning tax dollars to the citizens of her state. When John McCain introduced her as his running mate, the Republican Party seemed energized by her conservative, down-to-earth presence on the ticket.

Not everyone was enthusiastic about her, of course.

Without attempting to deal with the political tactics, strategies, and conniving, think about what you know about Sarah Palin. Whether you agree with her or not, ask yourself, *How smart is she?* Your answer is probably based largely on the *Saturday Night Live* humor: "I can see Russia from my house." She attended college in Idaho, and many pointed out how backwoods that was. In other words, right away Palin was marginalized by humor and definitions. Let me ask you this: Do you know her IQ? How would her score stack up against, say, Joe Biden's? Did you come to your conclusion numerically, on the basis that her gaffes outnumbered Biden's? If you did, please count again.

The truth is, we come to our decisions largely based on definitions—in Sarah Palin's case, these definitions were created largely by *Saturday Night Live*—and we define people quickly. We use such terms as *honest, trustworthy, homespun, intelligent, stupid, awkward, clumsy, dumb,* and on and on—many words the world would be better off without.

Assumptions

Think back to the show *Britain's Got Talent* and the appearance of Susan Boyle. This unattractive, disheveled, middle-aged woman walked onto the stage, and people in the audience tittered. Even the judges showed disrespect through their facial expressions and glances at each other. When she opened her mouth, however, the most glorious and mellifluous of sounds emerged. Ask yourself, *Why do I assume that a singer should look a certain way?* You might also ask, *Who sold that assumption to me, and why?*

Biases

Uncovering our biases is an important step in discovering ourselves. Evaluating the words we choose, what they mean, what they imply, and how we use them is an exercise in self-awareness. Whether we repeat a "blonde" joke, a sexist expectation, a racist definition, an age bias, or just the labels we put on one another, we deserve to think carefully about all that's implied and to question ourselves again: *Is that what I truly mean? Why?*

In *Mind Programming,* I recount a story told by Jesse Jackson. One evening while he was returning to his hotel, he heard rapidly approaching, heavy footsteps coming from behind. Growing anxious, he turned, saw a white man, and breathed a sigh of relief.[7] Imagine the humiliation of that moment for Reverend Jackson. How many such revelations could we all experience?

Practicing Your Character

What if you could relive your childhood? Would you create a different *you?* Remember when you practiced your character? Perhaps you were a romantic and practiced kissing your first sweetheart. Maybe you were an up-and-coming tough guy and stood in front of the mirror to practice lines such as "Go ahead. Make my day!" Possibly you wanted to be a model, so you practiced your walk.

The point is that we all rehearsed being what we thought it would be cool to be. As we practiced—something I've shown the power of in my book *Choices and Illusions*—our trained actions became automatic.[8] Things that are so habitual are no longer noticed by our attention and therefore enter our zone of beliefs. We come to believe ourselves to be something that's homemade, created by none other than ourselves.

What if you could have a redo on your scripting, your practicing? Would you change anything? What labels do you use to describe yourself? How do you put those labels on others?

Inconsistencies

In his children's book *The Little Soul and the Sun,* Neale Donald Walsch tells a story about a life before this life, where souls get together and plan coming into this world.[9] Imagine that you're a soul and for whatever reason, perhaps to learn about love, you choose to come to this world as a handicapped child—let's say one with Down syndrome. You choose a family because you know they'll love you despite your physical impairments; you choose the mother because you know she won't abort you. You're born and you're loved, but many mock your parents for allowing you to live. They question your mother's judgment. They make fun of you while donating to charities that support handicapped children, such as the Special Olympics.

Many of those who criticize your mother, ironically, are inspired by young people who have overcome their limitations to tell the rest of the world: "If I can do it—then you can as well!" How do you feel about those who mock your mother for her faith and love? Knowing that this scenario could be totally representative of Sarah Palin and her son Trig—does that influence your opinion of Palin?

Imagine you're still this little soul destined to come into the world handicapped. How do you feel when your mother decides to abort you?

Well, maybe there is no pre-life and no afterlife, but imagine you're a mother and you're told that you're pregnant with a child who has Down syndrome. What do you do? All of us make decisions every day based on our beliefs and our willingness to at least enter into a dialectic of sorts with ourselves while we mull the issue over and examine it from different perspectives.

Centenarians

I had a rude awakening in 2000. On an educational channel, I happened to catch a television special that was all about centenarians (those who have attained the age of 100 years or more). They were sharing stories of what it was like to be alive during the past 100 years, the whole of the 20th century. There were incredible tales, but I was taken aback by how young most of them seemed. I was seeing people who looked as if they were in their late 60s and early 70s, not ones who looked at all as if they were 100 or older—at least, not as I expected them to look.

Talk to teens and they'll almost unanimously tell you that 50 is old—and they don't want to get old. Yet if you ask, as I said earlier, "Who wants to live to be 100?" 99-year-olds will probably raise their hands. What do *you* expect a 100-year-old person to look like?

Self-Fulfilling Prophecies

Your expectation can become a self-fulfilling prophecy—and usually does. What if you knew that how you thought you'd look, feel, and get around at a given age actually predicted more or less what was coming? Would you make any changes to your expectations? Would you rewrite your definition of *old?* Would you find more use for people in their 70s, 80s, 90s, and older? At what age do you honestly think the ability to contribute to society ends? Does it ever? Do you feel at all different today from the way you felt when you were younger?

Our biases are bound by definitions, and most are hidden from our attention unless we actively seek them out. Research suggests that such little things as what I expect of myself when I'm older do indeed affect what actually happens. In fact, the data shows that age can be reversed, simply by fully remembering youth, so that you feel it and see it in your mind's eye. Change the definition and you become younger.

My book *Choices and Illusions* discusses levitation and hypnosis. The punch line is that levitation was common in hypnosis until the definition of our world changed through the spread of Newtonian physics. Once everyone became "knowledgeable" and knew that heavy matter (bodies) didn't float, levitation became uncommon.[10] I wonder what else has become rare. Do you?

What if you believed that you could float upward in the air—would you? Could you? What else might you do if you believed you could? What if *belief* creates your world?

✧✧✧

chapter 22

Growing Up

*"Tell me what gives a man or woman their greatest
pleasure and I'll tell you their philosophy of life."*

— ATTRIBUTED TO DALE CARNEGIE

When I was young, I wanted to become a man just
as soon as I could. It's amusing to me now, for today I
see the man as just a different version of the boy. Indeed,
one of my favorite sayings is: "The principal difference
between a man and a boy is the price of his toys." How
true! That observation, of course, is through the lens of
20/20 hindsight.

Where I come from, being a man rather than a boy
meant being rugged and tough and knowing. There
would be stages to go through. At age 12, I was deemed
old enough to pay some room and board to my parents.
At 15, I could buy my first car and drive on a work per-
mit. At 16, I was free to drive anywhere, at any time of
day. At 18, well, I was almost there. Reaching the age of
21 was anticlimactic. I'd already been in the bars and
done the things teenagers of my generation dreamed of

doing. And along the way were other unspoken rites of passage, such as owning my first gun.

Being a Man

It was exciting to go hunting; it was a man's sport. Killing a big deer, an elk, or some other animal was not only a hobby, but food for the family—ah, but was it? I remember well calculating the cost of my rifle, ammunition, license, trip into the backcountry, and so on, only to discover that the cost of venison was much higher per pound than that of beef in the grocery store. Maybe it's not that way for everyone, but I imagine that the cost differential is even greater today than years ago when I did the math.

Of course, some could argue that I used the gun for many years, so the full price shouldn't be factored into the cost of the first deer. But as I remember, even when I removed that item from my equation, it was still cheaper to buy food in the store if my time was worth anything. Therefore, the hunt had to have been about power, fun, joy, and the kill. Today I can think of nothing that's less fun than going hunting—and I'm sure I'm more *grown up* today than back then.

Why does society treasure killing? From video games to an actual hunt for wild game, why are young people so enthralled by taking lives? Why does our society promote this as a part of growing up? Older cultures may have depended on their warriors and hunters, but do we? Is it even possible to advance world peace while you sponsor killing—virtual or otherwise—even if only tacitly?

What if I'd wanted to be a cheerleader for my high school? There wasn't any such thing as a male cheerleader when I was young, so that desire would have led to all kinds of name calling. Nevertheless, despite our advances, stereotypes still exist.

When anthropologists and historians look at older cultures, they make judgments about the nature of their societal practices, the games, traditions, stories, myths, and so forth. What will they write about us 200 years from now—or 2,000 years from now? Will humanity still exist that far off?

Primitive Desires

We live at a time when our technology, awareness, and information flow make it possible for us to immediately view the grossest of actions and the latest in research. More than ever before, our culture has the opportunity to choose the direction it wants to take. As informed and educated as we are, we know what should be done—so why don't we do it? Or do we?

The primitive nature of our species often dominates our so-called higher-brain evolution. This is as true of sex as it is of violence. Young women must have a certain look, dress a certain way, present themselves according to certain standards of appearance, and on and on. The amount of cosmetic surgery performed today is alarming. More and more stories like that of reality star Heidi Montag surface. In case you don't remember, Heidi, who starred in MTV's *The Hills,* admitted to having gone through ten such procedures in one day.

From breast augmentation to rhinoplasty, from Botox to liposuction, the rage to look a certain way arguably has swelled to near epidemic proportions. Why is that?

"Comfortable in my own skin" is an old expression that perhaps has more meaning today than ever. That said, the media, peers, marketers, and more create the myths that promote being inauthentic today. I find it amusing that a number of so-called spiritual people must resort to medical procedures (Botox, face peels, and the like) before they're comfortable with themselves. The old Sufi saying, "When you know the difference between the container and the contents, you know all," weighs on me. How have we allowed such distortions in our maturation process, in our self-image, in our entertainment, and in our daydreams?

You Are Not Your Body

What if you realize that the you inside isn't the "vehicle" you're driving? Is it then as necessary to pose in that vehicle as it was before the realization? We polish our automobiles and often buy new ones (or at least new to us), and we love a sports car that's our pride and joy. Why not give the same attention to our bodies? That's the argument I've heard from some.

Taking care of the body, I submit, isn't the same as remodeling it. I can accept that there may be times when it's appropriate to undergo "remodeling" surgery, such as correcting a deviated septum in order to breathe better. But that's different from responding to a fixation on how our appearance corresponds to the image sold to us by those who want us to buy their products.

Growing up isn't easy, but it seems to be compounded with difficulties today. That's true not just for our young people but for many adults who have never completed the maturation process. Indeed, can we say that we've fully matured when our mental disposition is that of a child, or when our sole ambition is to have what the rich and famous do? What happens when we discover that we don't know nearly as much as we think we do, or when we chase an image that insists we do anything except accept ourselves as we are?

What if we never grow up? What if life is a process that never ends—it only changes or shifts from one to another? Do we ever mature?

chapter 23

Meaning: It's All a Simulation

"There is a popular cliché . . . which says that you cannot get out of computers any more than you put in. Other versions are that computers only do exactly what you tell them to, and that therefore computers are never creative. This cliché is true only in a crashingly trivial sense, the same sense in which Shakespeare never wrote anything except what his first schoolteacher taught him to write—words."

— RICHARD DAWKINS

What if Nick Bostrom, Oxford professor of philosophy, was correct when he considered the possibility that some very advanced civilization might create a simulation with intelligent beings, albeit artificially intelligent beings, that inhabited it. Assume, as he did, that there were no moral contrarians to oppose the simulation.[1] It may have been done originally as an experiment or as just some sort of game. Perhaps, in this theoretical advanced civilization, there was a development that led to simulating artificial life, or *alife,* as developed and named by American computer scientist Christopher Langton. (He came up with the term in the late '80s when he set up the first International Conference on the Synthesis and Simulation of Living Systems, also known as Artificial Life, at Los Alamos National Laboratory.)[2]

If Bostrom is correct, the probability is much higher that we're living a simulation than that we'd be the civilization that created the model. What if we inhabit a simulated universe, and our life itself is a simulation? How would we know or discover that?

Bostrom's famous argument, simplified, goes like this:

1. It's possible that an advanced civilization could create a computer simulation that contains individuals with artificial intelligence (AI).

2. Such a civilization would likely run many of these simulations, billions for example (just for fun, for research, or for any other permutation of possible reasons).

3. A simulated individual wouldn't necessarily know that it's inside a simulation—it's just going about its daily business in what it considers to be the "real world."

Then the ultimate question is—if one accepts that these premises are at least possible—which of the following is more likely?

a. We're the one civilization that develops AI simulations and happens not to be inside of one.

b. We're one of the many (billions) of simulations that have run. (Remember point 3.)

In greater detail, his argument attempts to prove the trichotomy that one of three situations is true:

1. Intelligent races will never reach a level of technology where they can run simulations of reality so detailed that they can be mistaken for reality (assuming that this is possible in principle).

2. Races who do reach such a sophisticated level don't tend to run such simulations.

3. We're almost certainly living in such a simulation.[3]

Endless, Ever-Expanding Universe

So imagine: What if you're a form of artificial intelligence that has evolved over what you believe is a few million years, and all of this has happened within a synthetic environment—your world as you know it? Because it's all created, the designers could provide for what might seem to be an endless, ever-expanding universe. There would be the rules that you live by, such as those we know from Newtonian physics; and then there would be the rule set that controls the finer detail, the so-called subatomic, the quantum.

Since one rule set is built for you to play in, and you may never have been meant to discover the other rules, the peculiar way in which waves manifest themselves as particles and vice versa isn't so extraordinary. Indeed, the entire idea of an uncertainty principle is easily understood. Of course the act of observation changes the simulation, for the simulation rule set is dynamic and dependent only on what's explored, examined, and believed by the players—the artificial intelligence in the simulation.

Indeed, the so-called alife modifies the rule set as it progresses. It would be designed this way so that the alife forms would have the ability to evolve, just as we know the evolution of our species in our world—real or otherwise.

Many Worlds

In the simulation, one's worldview would become, in a sense, one's reality. Perception would be driven by underlying beliefs, and therefore expectations. Given this programming, many worlds could simultaneously exist, albeit independent of one another from the standpoint of direct perception.

As such, say that under Condition 1, you have two lovers, you choose one to be your lifelong partner, and you live out this life. In another dimension, a so-called parallel world, another *you* would choose the other lover and live out that life under Condition 2. The program would have to allow for this alternative-choice function in order to anticipate all possible choices, conditions, and outcomes. Like a data rule set governing a computer program, your choices would be in the alternative, and the programmer would anticipate this. If the choice is X, then use Y rule; but if X sub one, then YY, and so on. Those in the simulations would perhaps think of this as the multiple-world hypothesis—as we do our world.

Miracles

Continuing, so-called miracles would really be exceptions to the rule. A character is to experience X and Y, and no event can alter that. So if—in theory—something were to happen that could or should lead to the death of the character, the program doesn't let it happen, and the character lives on.

Some characters, for such purposes as research but unknown to the characters themselves, are reborn. Sometimes they remember events from prior existences within the simulation, and, ergo, reincarnation theories blossom. Some characters die in one possible world outcome but continue in another; still others die, but their consciousness refuses to accept this rule, and they continue in a virtual environment created by their perceptions—a ghost world, or the famous *bardo* (Tibetan for "in-between world").

The Illusion

It's easy to see that, using the framework of a simulation, everything we experience or know in some sense in this world, anomalous and otherwise, can be easily explained. Perhaps at some time in history the original inhabitants knew more directly of this illusion, and so they called it just that. Escaping became their credo; and in time, some came to know this as a religious principle. Perhaps early lifespans were advanced enough to build civilizations that threatened the program, so they were eliminated—a kind of "start-over" was initiated. You can have a lot of fun with this, but where does it all lead?

Imagine that, as in the movie *The Matrix,* you discover that you're an alife. Does that change anything? What are your thoughts about the creator when you cast them in this light?

Would a world like this hold out hope for the survival of individual consciousness? Assume the designers built a sort of collective memory into the simulation and that each new alife arrived with the ability to tap into this, like the morphogenetic fields described by Rupert Sheldrake.[5] All alife might then appear to share certain archetypes, as well as benefit from the 100th-monkey effect (the theory that when a critical number of group members learn a new way of doing something, that this learning will spread spontaneously to everyone).[6] This is exactly the idea behind neural-net-based digital-organism simulators.

Today we have a variety of simulators that spawn life that evolves. A quick Google search of artificial-life simulators brings back notable results along with artificial-life software. These *creatures,* if that word is fitting, have complex DNA, usually Turing Complete. (In computability theory, a program is said to be Turing Complete when the rules followed in sequence on arbitrary data can produce the result of any calculation.)[7]

What would you do if you decided that this is all just an illusion—a simulation generated for whatever reason by some Grand Organizing Designer (GOD)? Would you do anything differently?

Wired to Be Good

Our species is wired to receive a natural reward when we help one another. Studies have repeatedly demonstrated that going to the aid of another gives rise to a neurological bath of "good-feeling" neurochemicals. When I consider the possibility that this is all just a simulation and ask myself what I'd do differently, I realize that as long as I dedicate my life to helping others, it doesn't much matter in a pragmatic sense.

However, there are those who would seize the opportunity to maximize their pleasure in whatever way they could, or so say some of the more fundamentalist arguments when considering the possibility that the world might end up being atheistic. This is highly possible, considering the current science and teachings that laugh at and omit various creation theories from our public-education system. What are your thoughts? If it were all just a simulation, what would you do? What would you believe? How would your life be different? Think about the commandments, the admonishments, and any other parameters that you've chosen to live by—would anything change?

It might all be just a simulation. If there's a model of this type anywhere, as we noted in the beginning, it's more likely that we're the alife forms than those who would or could create such a thing.

I wonder—will a simulation within a simulation ever be built? Or has it already happened? What if we're living in that inner world—does that change anything for you? In a way, isn't this either all there is and will ever be or a simulation, for our eternal nature will indeed, at some point, exit the so-called corporeal illusion?

Have you thought of life this way? What if you did— what then?

chapter 24

The Little Lie

"Disingenuous is the most honest word I know."

— ATTRIBUTED TO CARL STOYNOFF

Imagine that you're a university student who works nights and weekends at a coffee shop. Your manager wants you to stop brewing decaffeinated coffee because the demand is low and most of it gets thrown out. (You're required to make fresh coffee every hour.) It's almost closing time, and in walks a customer who orders an extra-large decaf. You tell him that you'll have to brew it, which could take five minutes. He agrees to wait and goes to the restroom. You think for a moment, then fill that extra-large cup with regular coffee. Why not? He'll never know the difference, and why waste a full pot of decaffeinated?

Your customer picks up his coffee. He adds an artificial sweetener, tastes it, then asks you, looking for reassurance, "Is this decaf?" What else can you tell him? You nod *yes,* and he leaves.

The weekend passes quickly, and Monday you're back in school. A friend of yours is distraught and leaving the campus as you arrive.

"What's wrong?" you ask.

"My father had a heart attack driving back home after coming out to see me this past weekend," he answers. Your friend continues, "He must have been really tired, for they say his caffeine level was really high and that, together with his tiredness, probably triggered the attack. He knows better, so he's always careful to order decaf."

You flash back to the weekend and the switch you made. You ask, "Are you telling me that one cup of coffee caused the heart attack?"

"I don't know. It was probably just the proverbial last straw on the camel's back. The doctors think he could have survived the heart attack, but he lost control of the car, and the accident killed him."

Now think for a minute. This scenario could really happen. If it did, how would you feel? It all started with just one fib—a tiny stretch of the truth. Who would ever expect such a result from a simple attempt to avoid waste? One little lie—is that so wrong?

Think back to the philosophical nature of the problem you examined earlier. Imagine that you're summoned to the hospital because both your parents were in an automobile accident. Your father was killed instantly; your mother is in intensive care and asking for him. The physician instructs you not to upset your mom. Her recovery is fragile at the moment, so whatever you do, you mustn't let her know that your father is dead. Doing so could kill her, you're told. The first thing your mother does is ask about your father, and of course you lie. It's well intentioned and meant to save a life.

A Reason to Lie

Is that the difference—the reason for the lie? It's okay to save a life versus wasting some coffee? Can you really know in advance what you should do? What if the doctor doesn't warn you, so you tell your mother of your father's death? She gasps, appears to choke, has a massive heart attack, and dies. The stressful news is just too much for her body to handle. Are you to blame?

The consequences of our actions can and often do have multiple ramifications. Imagine that a person comes to the door of a home and asks many questions. Mom tells him about her business selling products related to his inquiries. He wants to know more, so she takes a business catalog belonging to her young son and hands it to the stranger. The boy objects because it's his catalog—his father gave it to him. She assures the child that she has another one and will get it for him. It turns out, however, that there's no other catalog, and the boy never forgets the incident. Does it matter whether Mom was honestly mistaken or that she wanted to get rid of the caller by using her son's catalog? Does it matter to the boy? After several years the trust bond may be rebuilt, but is it ever really complete?

How often do you let a falsehood fly? Maybe someone asks a simple question, such as: "Did you have a good weekend?" You've just had a horrible argument with your significant other. Do you answer truthfully, or do you fib?

Stretching the truth may be habit forming. My research shows that people who exaggerate, hide themselves from others, and compensate for insecurities or feelings of inferiority are often less than completely honest. Think about yourself and those you know. How often is the truth stretched at least a little?

"So what?" you might ask. "Does it matter?" Tiny lies—do they make a difference? Do they accumulate and damage character? Obviously, not all fibs lead to someone's death, so when is it okay to lie?

Partial Truths

For years, I conducted lie-detection tests—in all, more than a thousand. One of the setup statements I always made went like this: "Now, you're here to tell me the truth today, right? And you understand the truth does not know percentages. That is, it is the whole truth, not a partial truth, not some percentage of the truth. I mean, would you like your mate to be 99 percent faithful?"

The point is clear. In this context, we understand that truth is not divisible—it is either the truth (the whole truth) or it isn't. What if you decided that you were going to tell the truth from now on unless it was to protect someone?

Let's assume you make that decision. Then a family member comes to you and admits a mistake. It's a felony, but it's not a violent crime. In fact, it's a victimless crime, at least from the standpoint of who got hurt. You live in a state that has a *misprision of felony* statute, which means if you conceal the felony, you commit one yourself. What do you do? Do you hide the truth and protect your loved one, or tell the truth and keep your word to yourself—that you'd be honest?

The Bible doesn't say, "Thou shalt not lie." What it does say is: "Thou shalt not bear false witness against thy neighbor." So is an untruth that isn't about my neighbor also a lie? Is falsehood inherently wrong? Is it wrong at all? If so, when? When is a tall tale truly a lie? Under what circumstances is an outright lie immoral?

Political Tactics

Politicians stretch the truth all the time. President George H. W. Bush probably lost his reelection bid because he said, "Read my lips—no new taxes!" Then he raised taxes. President Bill Clinton is infamous for saying: "I did not have sexual relations with that woman!" Later he equivocated on the definition of sexual relations in order to avoid charges of perjury—a bad idea, and one that didn't work, either. Hillary Clinton's Presidential campaign said that she hit the ground running during a visit to Iran, implying that she was under fire from the enemy, while the truth was quite different. When is a lie a gaffe, and when is it a premeditated prevarication that should be condemned?

In our judicial system we prosecute people for perjury. The former queen of household items for Kmart, Martha Stewart, was found guilty of perjury—not insider trading or some other serious matter. She was used to send a message to others and wound up with a severe sentence. A small lie in the courtroom is a crime. So is it always wrong to lie?

Who's Lying?

Think about how many times you've judged a person based on a misstatement (perhaps you just called it a lie). You probably forgave it, even found justification for it, if you were favorably disposed toward the person telling the untruth. And you probably went the other way if you weren't in that person's corner.

This is very obvious with our politicians. The one you support can make a mistake, which is at its worst a gaffe, while the one you oppose is simply a liar. President Barack Obama promised that the work of Congress would be open, with no closed-door deals, and we would see it all on C-SPAN. However, majority leader Senator Harry Reid and majority leader Representative Nancy Pelosi went behind closed doors and made outrageous deals; and when C-SPAN itself clamored for open hearings, the President ignored the message. Those who'd supported him dismissed those actions as meaning nothing. After all, Pelosi herself said something along the lines of: "Well, many things are said on the campaign trail," implying that everybody stretches the truth when trying to win the vote. So when do you want to hold an elected official accountable?

Many people tell their children not to lie, and then they cheat (lie) on their taxes. Perhaps the phone rings and you don't want to answer it, so you ask your mate to tell the caller you're not home. Your children hear this conversation and ask, "Why are you lying?" Did you just teach them to disregard the truth?

Clearly, there's no hard-and-fast rule about when lying may or may not be acceptable. What there can be is self-awareness of the degree to which we personally hold the standard of total truth to be inviolate. Hopefully, we then apply that standard, whatever it might be, fairly to all situations. What if you could make a rule about lying—what would it be?

chapter 25

Discernment

*"Wisdom is your perspective on life, your sense
of balance, your understanding of how the various parts
and principles apply and relate to each other. It embraces
judgment, discernment, comprehension. It is a gestalt
or oneness, and integrated wholeness."*

— STEPHEN R. COVEY

What does it mean to be human? Is it reflected
in our awareness of being conscious? We have a self-
identity; we're capable of future planning and reason;
we separate ourselves from the rest of the animal world
by wrongly placed arrogation or because we prize our
mental prowess above that of other creatures. Indeed,
the animal kingdom has many species that can outrun
us or outperform us physically. Some have opposable
digits on their hands, some build tools, and a few can
even learn our language and sign it back to us. So all
in all, we devise our system of definitions to say that
the human, the Homo sapiens, is superior because of
consciousness.

We highly prize the mind, the brain, consciousness, and all of its abilities. We sometimes make decisions about life and death based on mental acuity alone, as with a famous case from 2005 that I'll cover in more detail after this thought experiment (which is based upon it).

Imagine that you have a loved one, perhaps a daughter, who's in a permanent vegetative state caused by a blow to the head. She lies in bed day after day, with a feeding tube supplying her needs for liquid and nutrition. With this device, she maintains breathing and normal blood pressure unassisted. You visit daily for years and the doctors see no progress. Sometimes you ask her questions and swear up and down that she's aware and conscious. You call in a specialist, who determines that she isn't vegetative and isn't in a coma. The doctors disagree. More of them are prepared to say she is vegetative, as if numbers counted. You're encouraged to unplug the feeding tube and let her go—death by starvation and/or dehydration. What do you do?

Aware but Unable

Imagine that you're the one considered permanently vegetative. You lie in bed aware but unable to move, unable to reply or even gesture. You work at finding some way to let the outside world know that you're still here—still in the body. Slowly, over several years, you gain some ability to smile, to track a balloon with your eyes, to open and close your eyelids on command, and you try hard to do what's asked of you. Still, the physicians believe the movement is coincidental and means nothing; the eye closures are considered reflexive. According to most of your physicians, you're permanently vegetative, which means *forever*. Imagine how you might feel. Imagine your sadness and hopelessness, perhaps even the pure depression and unwillingness even to try. Feel how all of this and more might overtake you emotionally. But there you are, a prisoner in your immobile body.

Let's assume another consultant advises against unplugging the tube or withdrawing treatment for infections. They urge that this should happen only when there's also a flat-line EEG, a positive apnea test (cessation of breathing), or a lack of brain blood flow on transcranial Doppler or by angiography—any of which would make your state more certainly vegetative.

Unplugged

Now, still as the patient, imagine that your husband has told everyone you'd want to be unplugged and insists on disconnecting you. Your parents oppose this action in every possible way because, having spent endless hours with you, they're convinced that you're aware. The matter becomes a court case, and money is an issue as well. A lawsuit has been filed, and your husband claims that your life expectancy is at least another 50 years, so a medical-malpractice award for not treating you earlier with something—anything—should entitle the two of you to $20 million to cover the cost. Nothing is said at this trial about your desire to be unplugged. The result is a cash award—say, $1.5 million. Now your husband remembers that you'd want to be unplugged if anything like this happened. Does this influence how you feel about the whole matter?

Information Available

Now let's imagine that you're unrelated to the situation. You've read and heard the reports, and the doctors are saying two different things. You'll come to some decision in your mind about what you think should be done, if only tentatively, based on limited information. If you think about it, your choice will be colored by what you'd want to happen if the person were you. Is that the right way to make the call? Would your decision be the same if the person were your child?

The Evidence

Okay, let's soup up the mix, to use some hot-rod talk. It's two years later, and research begins to pour out. Headlines enter the mainstream media: "Giving the Unconscious a Voice" and "Vegetative Brains Show Signs of Awareness." The articles discuss new technology and methods, and the result shows that many diagnosed as being in a permanent vegetative state are in fact able to respond to specific questions. These patients can answer *yes* or *no* by imagining the answer, and specialists watch the appropriate area of the brain respond, indicating that the question was understood.

Let's assume you pushed for the person to be unplugged from the feeding tube, to die by starvation. How do you feel now? On the other hand, assume you were the person's parent, who fought the unplugging of the feeding tube. How do you feel?

Can you imagine realizing, in 20/20 hindsight, that you'd watched your child die of starvation and dehydration, and all the while, when she looked at you, she was aware of what was happening?

What if you could do something about this? What if you could ensure that it never happened to another person? Would you do anything? Would you want to? Would a spiritually advanced person do more (or less) than one who didn't care at all about this situation? Is giving lip service to something the same as taking action?

Terri Schiavo

You may have recognized similarities between this scenario and the real case of Terri Schiavo. If you don't know Terri's story beyond the thought experiment you just completed, I can tell you that her parents contested her husband's right to have Terri's life terminated. Her husband argued that her wish would be to end it rather than continue to live as she was, sustained by a feeding tube. Her parents argued that she was still aware, and that her Roman Catholic upbringing would never allow her to want to end her own life. A friend testified that she knew Terri wouldn't want the feeding tube disconnected because she disapproved of such things after watching a television movie about Karen Ann Quinlan, whose parents took their comatose daughter off her respirator. (The friend's testimony was discredited on the basis of timing issues.)

Learn All the Facts

Okay, history is history. The account, including the money side of it, is available online, and I strongly recommend that you read the entire story.[1] The breakthroughs in treatment as set out in the articles "Giving the Unconscious a Voice" and "Vegetative Brains Show Signs of Awareness" are also true. [2, 3] So as I say, it's all history now, but perhaps it will be important for someone tomorrow. In our thought experiment, you made a decision. What did you decide? You're becoming the product of your choices!

Judging is different from discernment. When doing the former, I decide between alternatives, such as right and wrong, but each of us must discern for ourselves the path we will walk. Making wise decisions calls for a level of discernment that goes beyond who's right and who's wrong. The story of King Solomon determining which of two women was a child's true mother by offering to cut the child in two shows us that wisdom—discernment—is much more than judgment. In this instance, he discerned which woman would be best at mothering, not necessarily who the biological parent was. Therefore, his aim wasn't entirely to judge who was telling the truth. We'd like to think that the biological mother was the one willing to give up her claim to protect the child, but real life tells us that this may not be the case.

What if our world leaders were truly wise—would the world be any different? Is there a test for wisdom? Could we elect someone based on such an exam? How do you think you'd score if you took the discernment test? Shades of grey, not black or white—what if that's all there ever is?

chapter 26

The Unexamined Life

"The unexamined life is not worth living."

— SOCRATES

If you've read my earlier book *What Does That Mean? Exploring Mind, Meaning, and Mysteries,* you know that above all else, I hold the search for understanding the self to be a virtue. I believe that in our modern society, there's too much emphasis on copying others and too little time given to self-discovery.

Human beings are great mimics. We've been known to join in having symptoms of some hysterical illness brought about only by suggestion and imitation.[1] We've put on a prison guard's uniform and changed our personality and values, tortured, and humiliated prisoners.[2] We've stood by and depended on others to stop or report a crime or even to go to the aid of a victim struck by an automobile. [3, 4]

In fact, we've been known to shift blame and to imitate self-control—or the lack of it—according to the behavior of those around us. Research shows that just thinking about someone with little self-control weakens our own. We watch someone choose a cookie from a plate that holds both cookies and carrots, and most of us are led to eat cookies ourselves.[5] The super merchandisers, such as the neuro-marketers (those who use the latest neurological devices such as fMRI and PET to evaluate live responses to stimuli), know all this and use advanced methods to learn more about us. There are those in what should be called the "media-ocracy" and others who use our worst qualities against us.[6]

Society

We grow up to join the world of consumption, full of wishes and dreams that typically include big houses, fancy automobiles, lots of money, and ample time for recreation. Our value systems have shifted from being more or less absolute to being culturally relevant. Our ideas of self-reliance are often invested in what others can and will do for us. Our authentic selves are lost to the counterfeit selves now intent on maximizing pleasure and minimizing pain. We know what we want, what we'll buy, what our goals are, and so on, but we don't know ourselves. We've memorized sound bites, and we use slogans to label our ideas so we don't get even, we get "evener." Our bumper stickers reflect our attitude: "Life sucks and then you die" or "TGIF." The passion in our lives has been surrendered to the same old, same old.

Being Original

My favorite question nowadays is this: "What was your last truly original thought?" It is always followed by silence. Think about it: Everything from your favorite color to the way you walk and talk has been influenced by your culture and by association with something you like or dislike on the basis of acceptability. For example, it's hard to find a so-called rugged American male who maintains that his favorite color is pink. Parents choose blue for boys and pink for girls, and they do so because they've been convinced that those colors are gender appropriate. In this way, almost subliminally, we're the product of the beliefs of others. Listen to any conversation and you find talk of the news, politics, entertainment, movies, unemployment, prosperity, and on and on. Where in that conversation are the original human beings and their unique thoughts?

Friends

What if you were shipwrecked, like the FedEx employee played by Tom Hanks in the gripping movie *Castaway?* Alone on an island, Hanks invents a friend by painting a face on a volleyball and naming it Wilson, from the brand name on the ball. Toward the end of the film, Hanks panics when Wilson falls into the sea.

We're herd animals, and we do need social support, but do we require it so much that we take no time for self-reflection? When we were children, did we need to invent playmates in order to avoid ourselves, or, alternatively, were we learning about ourselves through our imaginary friends?

What would you do if you were shipwrecked on an island? Would you begin talking to yourself, making up friends, or could you spend time getting to really know yourself? Being alone is difficult for many—it's almost like forced solitary confinement. How long do you think you could be happy by yourself?

A Mirror of Ourselves

It's common in certain circles to hear that what we find offensive in others is often a characteristic in ourselves. In other words, people are mirrors. So the overbearing child who knows it all is just a reflection of the overbearing parent. Given this definition, it's easy to see how our friends and associates could be our best teachers, particularly those for whom we have no patience and whom we can't stand.

Assume for the moment that this saying is true. Do we use it to help ourselves, or do we avoid the truth by steering clear of people who accurately reflect who we really are? Would you go out of your way to be with someone who annoyed you from sunup to sundown so that you could learn about yourself, heal one aspect of your being, and become a better human as a result? Or would you avoid that person and thereby pretend to be in good shape, with no need of learning anything or testing your understanding of yourself?

Is it ever appropriate to get down in the mud of the world so that you can find the things that annoy you, the things that frighten you, and the people and beliefs you despise? Should you instead remove yourself from a distasteful environment to find a better one? Is what my mother used to tell me true? She always said, "Birds of a feather flock together."

Conflicting Views

Imagine you're in a verbally abusive relationship. Your partner is constantly undermining your value, calling you names, putting you down in front of others, and embarrassing you for no reason. You visit your religious leader, who reminds you that you promised to cherish your partner in sickness and in health. The cleric reminds you of your children and how important the family is to them. Divorce shouldn't be considered, or at best it should be the last possible alternative. He or she offers to counsel you both, but your partner won't hear of it. Your cleric offers to speak to your partner alone, and you leave. What do you do next?

Imagine that you go to your success coach, who tells you to get out of the verbally abusive environment—you deserve better. You remind your coach that he or she has taught you this mirror-image idea, and you ask if you wouldn't be better off remaining until you've worked out the problem or at least until the situation no longer bothers you. The coach is caught between two mutually exclusive alternatives and leaves the choice to you. What do you do?

Imagine you run into your friend, a psychologist, at the grocery store. You tell this person about the problem, and he or she encourages you to start family counseling. What do you do?

Let's assume you really love your spouse. That person has slowly grown ill and is now in constant pain and heavily medicated much of the time. The pain makes him or her angry at everyone and everything. You've been together for more than 20 years and have four or five children. Is your decision the same as it would be if you had no children? Would you still think that your partner was a mirror of you? Or were the first two decades of bliss the real mirror, and the present just a distortion due to illness? Is it both—a mirror at first and a mirror now?

How do we know what truly reflects us if we have no idea who we are? How do we expect to find ourselves when the last person we want to be alone with is our own self?

My Trip to the Desert

I was once encouraged to go into the desert alone and take nothing with me—no wallet, no ID, no money—just me, some water, and trail mix. At the time, I really didn't know much about the desert other than what I'd seen in movies or on television and what I'd read about. I was raised along the Rockies, so as a boy I'd spent a good deal of time in the mountains but never the desert. I suppose, in hindsight, the desert was suggested so that I wouldn't know what to expect. I would be out of my element.

When we're in unfamiliar surroundings, with strangers or all alone in an unknown environment, a certain innocence emerges from beneath the outward image we project. This tends to make us feel uncertain, and we're therefore able to see anew that we aren't what we project at all. My desert journey was most helpful, and I share most of it in my book *Simple Things and Simple Thoughts.*[7] What's important here is the idea that we might have to go to some lengths to get out of our own way in order to find ourselves.

Examine Your Life

Socrates' admonition regarding the unexamined life implies the necessity of investigating ourselves. Looking at what we've done, what we've experienced, what our thoughts have been, the people we've known, our innermost secrets, what we believe, who has influenced us and why, and so much more is requisite to understanding ourselves. There's great truth in the axiom "Know thyself."

What if you had the opportunity to really get to know yourself? Would you take it? We have that chance every day, but the question is, how many of us actually use it? What if we all dedicated some part of each day to knowing ourselves—would the world be different?

chapter 27

Conclusion: The Exam

"Character is both developed and revealed by tests, and <u>all</u> of life is a test. You are <u>always</u> being tested. God constantly watches your response to people, problems, success, conflict, illness, disappointment, and even the weather! He even watches the simplest actions such as when you open a door for others, when you pick up a piece of trash, or when you're polite toward a clerk or waitress."

— Rick Warren

What if you learned that the real purpose of life was the decisions and actions you take that have to do with all of these *What if?* scenarios? What if you discovered that you're here to learn to be a god? In other words, what if you came to understand that you're here to perfect your highest self—that quintessential potential that exists when the original spark of your being unites with the awareness of who you are? Let's assume for a moment that you're going to be the one who answers prayers. Which ones will you respond to? What's the right thing? Is there even a *right thing?*

Imagine that you're an impartial arbitrator, and your mission is to be just and equitable with all. In this process, you learn to be what Plato called a *philosopher king*. That is, you find out how to be truly wise and to make the correct decision all the time. How would you learn to do this?

Tending to Life's Lessons

Life is a school, as many have observed. Unfortunately, many more ignore what it has to teach. Actor and social commentator Will Rogers once said, "There is nothing so stupid as the educated man if you get him off the thing he was educated in." Is it possible that when we ignore what goes on around us—or when we fail to work through a problem and derive a satisfactory answer that we're willing to share, or when we keep quiet and don't speak up for fear of ostracism by those in power—that we're turning our backs on our education and the purpose of our being here in the first place?

"In the world but not of the world" is a popular saying among spiritual teachers of our day. How can you be in this world if you ignore the pain of others, the conflicts that divide people and nations, and similarly difficult subjects? What does it mean to be not of this world? I think this statement addresses the proposition that you're eternal and recognizes that you have nothing to fear. I don't think it means you should give up your learning while you're here and do nothing but pine for the other world, to let be what will be.

Thank you for staying with me in this journey of exploring *What if?* scenarios. The journey could be much longer, for there are hundreds, perhaps even thousands or tens of thousands, of such thought experiments that could be worked on. Like any good riddle, they each have a challenge inherent in them, but the purpose of this work is only to bring to your attention the possibility that the very nature of these and other scenarios is part and parcel of why we're here.

According to Murphy's fifth law of applied terror (one of Murphy's infamous laws, albeit less well known than his first), "If you are given a take-home exam, you will forget where you live." Life is definitely a take-home exam—and what each of us takes home depends somewhat on the clarity with which we've come to know ourselves.

I believe that the first law of being divinely human is "Know thyself." That's the ultimate challenge and the real quest, for no one else can lead you to where you're meant to be. I hope that these *What if?* thought experiments and scenarios have added to your knowledge of yourself. I also hope that they may have provoked a path of inquiry that will forever enrich you.

Epilogue

Where Do I Go from Here?

"Wisdom is knowing what to do next,
skill is knowing how to do it, and virtue is doing it."

— David Starr Jordan

The question put to me by some who previewed this book was a simple one: "So where do we go from here?" It's a simple question without a simple answer. Some questions don't have black or white responses, and I hope that by now you've discovered that taking a hard-and-fast position on anything is usually ill advised until you know all the circumstances involved. In other words, part of wisdom may well be knowing when to ask questions and listen instead of give answers and talk.

Imagine a final examination in a theology or philosophy class in which there's only one question and your essay answer amounts to at least 50 percent of your grade. Now imagine that the test gives you no context but just says: "In the beginning, God created the heaven and the earth. Discuss."

Okay, discuss this from what perspective? Christianity? Judaism? Jainism? Scientism? Buddhism? Do you discuss all of them? Knowing what the class has covered because you attended every day and read all the material would be helpful, but what if this was an honors class and only one *A* would be given? Further, what if the professor had instructed you to read outside the course and include that material in your work? It's easy to see that the more information you have about the nature of the question—such as its circumstances and context— the better prepared you'd be to offer an answer. But at the same time, having so much information can lead to what has been termed *paralysis by analysis*.

Take Responsibility

Life is like this kind of examination, except it's always an open-book test. You have access to the information necessary in this modern age more readily than ever before. Today, a few strokes on a keyboard bring you a world's worth of answers. Arguably, the great advantage to our information age is the accessibility of data. Given that access, why would any of us grab onto a sound bite spoken by our favorite politician, local minister, preferred news anchor, or some pundit pushing an agenda? In fact, the first question I think of when I hear a person express an opinion is: *What do they have to gain out of this?* You might be surprised (but you shouldn't be) by how few points of view are truly objective and free of agendas. That indeed is a part of our modern problem with the so-called news networks. Journalism today is more often opinion than unbiased reporting.

The days of the facts—only the facts and nothing but the facts—seem to have passed into history.

Be Wise

Clearly, the first thing to do on the journey is to be wise. That means you should investigate the alternatives and consider the options, weigh the reasons behind the arguments, and be willing to accept responsibility for your decisions as though you were actually ruling on the matter and yours would be the deciding word.

Gather Information

The next thing I encourage is developing and practicing the skills involved in gaining proper information and weighing the possibilities inherent in any proposition you consider. The best way I know to do that is to be informed, to gain reliable data. Just as an exercise, if you're a Democrat and love MSNBC, take time to watch Fox for an alternative view. If you're a Republican and love Fox, check out MSNBC for the other side of the story. Go out of your way to find the opposing perspectives regardless of the arena (politics, friends, work). Actively seek to understand viewpoints that differ from your own.

Develop the Skills

It's fair to ask: How do skills and information differ? The ability to make an informed choice is dependent upon finding the correct data. Such skills as decision making, information gathering, truth finding, establishing some hierarchy of significance, and selecting sources are all necessarily linked to resource information. Where they're different, they aren't entirely independent; and as with any skill, the more you practice, the more accomplished you become.

Separate Feeling from Facts

I suggest that another useful skill is separating feelings from facts. This can be harder to develop; nevertheless, it's necessary. We all too easily—and too often—find our decisions influenced by an attractive person, a charismatic leader, a good sales pitch, confused or conflated data, or the majority view. Remember the old political-science idea that all politicians begin with a popular truism such as "Taxes are too high"? It's an appealing statement and meets with general agreement. It might more properly be phrased "Lend me your ear," for it's designed to get your attention and win agreement at the same time. Next comes the second premise and then the conclusion, as though arguing with the logic of a syllogism. So, taxes are too high, the last administration has done *xyz* to worsen the situation, and therefore elect me because I'll do it differently. There will be change—or is it "Change we can count on"?

These arguments can seem compelling, and when they're delivered by someone we find attractive, our emotions often cloud our judgment. Just remember that truth and look behind the curtain. Wishing that the person could be who you want them to be doesn't make it so.

Take the Risk

Doing the right thing isn't always easy; sometimes you must buck the wishes of the crowd and in doing so risk your security. It's as important to stand up for your decision as it is to make it. Voice your opinion once you've done the homework and come to your conclusion. Share it, based on the facts, and do so without attachment to an outcome. In other words, offer information without needing to win anything.

All too often people disagree, and the difference of opinion becomes emotional. When that happens, all arguments are lost. No one gains from such an exchange. Have the virtue to know how and why you've come to your decision and share it with skill, not irrational emotion. You can be convincing—even somewhat emotional or passionate in your premises and conclusion—without offending or directly challenging another person in an aggressive manner.

Open Your Mind

Practice being open-minded, and remain that way. Try figuratively to walk a mile in the other person's shoes so that you can see or measure both sides of an issue. Think of your decisions as though they'll carry the day, and make them with proper prudence.

By being willing to look closely at what's at stake, you're really examining yourself. I believe that you'll find you're quite dynamic. There are few static views that rigidly refuse to respond to genuine and thoughtful inquiry. In this way, I think we wake up—a little bit at a time. We all learn more and more about ourselves—and perhaps our purpose—by observing our role in what Shakespeare called "the play," for it may be true in an eternal sense that life is but a passing scene.

Enjoy

You're a character in the play. What do you think of this person? Look up at the character on the stage from time to time. Use your imagination to see that you're playing yourself, but view it from the perspective of the audience. Imagine yourself to be both observer and actor. How do you want your character to behave? What if you could write the script? Would you change any of the lines?

You have the script in your hands—enjoy the play!

✧✧✧

Appendix

The Universal Declaration of Human Rights

Article 1

All human beings are created free and equal in dignity and rights. They are endowed with reason and conscience and should act towards one another in a spirit of brotherhood.

Article 2

Everyone is entitled to all the rights and freedoms set forth in this Declaration, without distinction of any kind, such as race, colour, sex, language, religion, political or other opinion, national or social origin, property, birth or other status. Furthermore, no distinction shall be made on the basis of the political, jurisdictional or international status of the country or territory to which a person belongs, whether it be independent, trust, non-self-governing or under any other limitation of sovereignty.

Article 3

Everyone has the right to life, liberty and security of person.

Article 4

No one shall be held in slavery or servitude; slavery and the slave trade shall be prohibited in all their forms.

Article 5

No one shall be subjected to torture or to cruel, inhuman or degrading treatment or punishment.

Article 6

Everyone has the right to recognition everywhere as a person before the law.

Article 7

All are equal before the law and are entitled without any discrimination to equal protection of the law. All are entitled to equal protection against any discrimination in violation of this Declaration and against any incitement to such discrimination.

Article 8

Everyone has the right to an effective remedy by the competent national tribunals for acts violating the fundamental rights granted him by the constitution or by law.

Article 9

No one shall be subjected to arbitrary arrest, detention or exile.

Article 10

Everyone is entitled in full equality to a fair and public hearing by an independent and impartial tribunal, in the determination of his rights and obligations and of any criminal charge against him.

Article 11

Everyone charged with a penal offence has the right to be presumed innocent until proved guilty according to law in a public trial at which he has had all the guarantees necessary for his defence.

No one shall be held guilty of any penal offence on account of any act or omission which did not constitute a penal offence, under national or international law, at the time when it was committed. Nor shall a heavier penalty be imposed than the one that was applicable at the time the penal offence was committed.

Article 12

No one shall be subjected to arbitrary interference with his privacy, family, home or correspondence, nor to attacks upon his honour and reputation. Everyone has the right to the protection of the law against such interference or attacks.

Article 13

Everyone has the right to freedom of movement and residence within the borders of each state.

Everyone has the right to leave any country, including their own, and to return to their country.

Article 14

Everyone has the right to seek and to enjoy in other countries asylum from persecution.

This right may not be invoked in the case of prosecutions genuinely arising from non-political crimes or from acts contrary to the purposes and principles of the United Nations.

Article 15

Everyone has the right to a nationality.

No one shall be arbitrarily deprived of his nationality nor denied the right to change his nationality.

Article 16

Men and women of full age, without any limitation due to race, nationality or religion, have the right to marry and to found a family. They are entitled to equal rights as to marriage, during marriage and at its dissolution.

Marriage shall be entered into only with the free and full consent of the intending spouses.

The family is the natural and fundamental group unit of society and is entitled to protection by society and the State.

Article 17

Everyone has the right to own property alone as well as in association with others.

No one shall be arbitrarily deprived of his property.

Article 18

Everyone has the right to freedom of thought, conscience and religion; this right includes freedom to change his religion or belief, and freedom, either alone or in community with others and in public or private, to manifest his religion or belief in teaching, practice, worship and observance.

Article 19

Everyone has the right to freedom of opinion and expression; this right includes freedom to hold opinions without interference and to seek, receive and impart information and ideas through any media and regardless of frontiers.

Article 20

Everyone has the right to freedom of peaceful assembly and association.

No one may be compelled to belong to an association.

Article 21

Everyone has the right to take part in the government of their country, directly or through freely chosen representatives.

Everyone has the right of equal access to public service in their country.

The will of the people shall be the basis of the authority of government; this will shall be expressed in periodic and genuine elections which shall be by universal and equal suffrage and shall be held by secret vote or by equivalent free voting procedures.

Article 22

Everyone, as a member of society, has the right to social security and is entitled to realization, through national effort and international co-operation and in accordance with the organization and resources of each State, of the economic, social and cultural rights indispensable for his dignity and the free development of his personality.

Article 23

Everyone has the right to work, to free choice of employment, to just and favourable conditions of work and to protection against unemployment.

Everyone, without any discrimination, has the right to equal pay for equal work.

Everyone who works has the right to just and favorable remuneration ensuring for himself and his family an existence worthy of human dignity, and supplemented, if necessary, by other means of social protection.

Everyone has the right to form and to join trade unions for the protection of his interests.

Article 24

Everyone has the right to rest and leisure, including reasonable limitation of working hours and periodic holidays with pay.

Article 25

Everyone has the right to a standard of living adequate for the health and well-being of himself and of his family, including food, clothing, housing and medical care and necessary social services, and the right to security in the event of unemployment, sickness, disability, widowhood, old age or other lack of livelihood in circumstances beyond his control.

Motherhood and childhood are entitled to special care and assistance. All children, whether born in or out of wedlock, shall enjoy the same social protection.

Article 26

Everyone has the right to education. Education shall be free, at least in the elementary and fundamental stages. Elementary education shall be compulsory. Technical and professional education shall be made generally available and higher education shall be equally accessible to all on the basis of merit.

Education shall be directed to the full development of the human personality and to the strengthening of respect for human rights and fundamental freedoms. It shall promote understanding, tolerance and friendship among all nations, racial or religious groups, and shall further the activities of the United Nations for the maintenance of peace.

Parents have a prior right to choose the kind of education that shall be given to their children.

Article 27

Everyone has the right freely to participate in the cultural life of the community, to enjoy the arts and to share in scientific advancement and its benefits.

Everyone has the right to the protection of the moral and material interests resulting from any scientific, literary or artistic production of which he is the author.

Article 28

Everyone is entitled to a social and international order in which the rights and freedoms set forth in this Declaration can be fully realized.

Article 29

Everyone has duties to the community in which alone the free and full development of his personality is possible.

In the exercise of his rights and freedoms, everyone shall be subject only to such limitations as are determined by law solely for the purpose of securing due recognition and respect for the rights and freedoms of others and of meeting the just requirements of morality, public order and the general welfare in a democratic society.

These rights and freedoms may in no case be exercised contrary to the purposes and principles of the United Nations.

Article 30

Nothing in this Declaration may be interpreted as implying for any State, group or person any right to engage in any activity or to perform any act aimed at the destruction of any of the rights and freedoms set forth herein.[1]

Endnotes

Introduction

1. Zimbardo, P. 2007. *The Lucifer Effect.* New York: Random House.

Chapter 1

1. Bach, R. 2009. *Hypnotizing Maria.* Newburyport, Mass.: Hampton Roads Publishing.

2. Wilson, T. D. 2002. *Strangers to Ourselves: Discovering the Adaptive Unconscious.* Cambridge, Mass.: Harvard University Press.

3. Ibid.

Chapter 3

1. Watson, R. 2007. *Cogito, Ergo Sum: The Life of Rene Descartes.* Boston, Mass.: David R. Godine.

2. Lacewing, M. 2010. *Descartes and the Method of Doubt.* http://cw.routledge.com/textbooks/philosophy /downloads/a2/unit4/descartes/DescartesDoubt.pdf

Chapter 4

1. Chen, S. 2009. "Gang Rape Raises Questions About By-standers' Role." http://www.cnn.com/2009/CRIME/10 /28/california.gang.rape.bystander/index.html

2. Wikipedia. "Murder of Kitty Genovese." http:// en.wikipedia.org/wiki/Kitty_Genovese

3. Wikipedia. "Kevin Carter." http://en.wikipedia.org /wiki/Kevin_Carter

4. Zimbardo, P. 2007. *The Lucifer Effect.* New York, N.Y.: Random House.

5. Grube, G. M. A., trans., and. Reeve, C. D. C. 1992. *Plato: Republic.* Cambridge, Mass.: Hackett Publishing Co.

6. Taylor, E. 2009. "When Everything Changes, Change Everything with Neale Donald Walsch." http://www .eldontaylor.com/provocative-enlightenment-radio -show/2009-10-29-when-everything-changes-change -everything-with-neale-donald-walsch.html

7. Kant, I. 1965. *Immanuel Kant's Critique of Pure Reason.* New York, N.Y.: St. Martin's Press.

8. MacIntyre, A. C. 1984. *After Virtue: A Study in Moral Theory.* Second Edition. Notre Dame, Ind.: University of Notre Dame Press.

9. Abrams, J. 2009. "Planned Parenthood Director Quits After Watching Abortion on Ultrasound." http://www .foxnews.com/us/2009/11/02/planned-parenthood -director-quits-watching-abortion-ultrasound

10. Ibid.

11. Unknown. 2009. "Reproductive Privacy Act." *California Health and Safety Code.* Section 123460-123468, Article 2.5. http://law.justia.com/california/codes/2009 /hsc/123460-123468.html

Chapter 5

1. Anderson, C. A. and Gentile, D. A. "Violent Video Games: The Effects on Youth, and Public Policy Implications" in *Handbook of Children, Culture, and Violence.* Ed. Dowd, N. E., Singer, D. G., and Wilson, R. F. 2005. Thousand Oaks, Calif.: Sage Publications.

2. Unknown. 2009. "Effects of Video Game Playing on Children." *MediaWise.org.* http://www.mediafamily .org/facts/facts_effects.shtml

3. Brady, S. S. and Matthews, K. A. 2006. "Effects of Media Violence on Health-Related Outcomes Among Young Men." *Archives of Pediatrics & Adolescent Medicine.* 2006; 160:341–347.

4. Smyth, J.M. 2007. "Beyond Self-Selection in Video Game Play: An Experimental Examination of the Consequences of Massively Multiplayer Online Role-Playing Game Play." *CyberPsychology & Behavior.* 10:717–721. http:// liebertonline.com/doi/abs/10.1089/cpb.2007.9963

5. Gentile, D. A. 2009. "Video Games Affect the Brain—for Better and Worse." *The Dana Foundation.* http://dana .org/news/cerebrum/detail.aspx?id=22800

6. Ibid.

7. Jackson, H. 2004. "Research of the Effects of Television." http://www.labouroflove.org/tv-toys-&-technology /television/research-on-the-effects-of-television

8. Fast, N.J., and Tiedens, L.Z. 2010. "Blame Contagion: The Automatic Transmission of Self-Serving Attributions." *Journal of Experimental Social Psychology*, 46:97–106.

9. Piderman, K. 2010. "Forgiveness: Letting Go of Grudges and Bitterness." http://www.mayoclinic.com/health /forgiveness/MH00131

Chapter 6

1. Maslow, A. H. 1993. *The Farther Reaches of Human Nature.* New York, N.Y.: Penguin.

2. Dougherty, J. 2009. "For Some Seeking Rebirth, Sweat Lodge Was End." *The New York Times.* http://www .nytimes.com/2009/10/22/us/22sweat.html

3. Gumbel, A. 2009. "Death Valley." *The Guardian.* http://www.guardian.co.uk/world/2009/oct/22 /james-ray-sweat-lodge-death

4. Tang, R. 2009. "Three Die in AZ Sweat Lodge, Leader Faces Lawsuits." *LegalFish: The Daily Tackle.* http:// www.legalfish.com/TheDailyTackle/2009/11/10 /three-die-in-az-sweat-lodge-leader-faces-lawsuits

5. Anticult. 2006. "James Arthur Ray - Oprah is Personally to Blame for Him Being Famous." *Rickross.com.* http:// forum.rickross.com/read.php?12,77450,78971

6. King, J. 2009. "Sweat Lodge Survivor Files Lawsuit; Claims Ray Barred Escape Before She Passed Out." *Phoenix New Times.* http://blogs.phoenixnewtimes.com/valleyfever /2009/11/sweat_lodge_survivor_files_law.php#

Chapter 7

1. Dawkins, R. 2008. *The God Delusion.* Boston, Mass.: Mariner Books.

2. Nick Hugget. 2004. "Zeno's Paradoxes." *Stanford Encyclopedia of Philosophy.* http://plato.stanford.edu/entries /paradox-zeno

Chapter 8

1. Baird, M. 2003. "The Sport of Kings Can't Provide a Royal Ending for Derby Winner Ferdinand." Humane Society of the United States. http://www.hsus.org/pets /pets_related_news_and_events/the_sport_of_kings _cant_provide_a_royal_ending_for_derby_winner _ferdinand.html

2. Wikipedia. "Mirror Test." http://en.wikipedia.org/wiki /Mirror_test

3. Plotnik, J. M., et al., 2009. "Self-Recognition in the Asian Elephant and Future Directions for Cognitive Research with Elephants in Zoological Settings." *Zoo Biology,* 28, 1–13.

4. Sheridan, K. 2006. *Animals and the Afterlife.* Carlsbad, Calif.: Hay House, Inc.

Chapter 9

1. Dostoevsky, F. 2008. *Crime and Punishment.* New York, N.Y.: Oxford University Press.

2. Anderson, G. 2006. *Biological Influences on Criminal Behavior.* Boca Raton, Fla.: CRC Press.

3. Robinson-Riegler, G. L. and Robinson-Riegler, B. 2007. *Cognitive Psychology: Applying The Science Of The Mind* (2nd Edition). Upper Saddle River, N.J.: Allyn and Bacon.

4. Pinker, S. 2009. *How the Mind Works.* New York, N.Y.: W. W. Norton and Company.

5. Zimbardo, P. 2007. *The Lucifer Effect.* New York, N.Y.: Random House.

Chapter 10

1. Watson, R. 2007. *Cogito, Ergo Sum: The Life of Rene Descartes.* Boston, Mass.: David R. Godine.

2. The Bible. Matthew 13:9, 15–16.

3. James, W. 1884. "What is an Emotion?" *Mind*: 9, 34. 188–205.

4. Siegel, D. J. 2007. *The Mindful Brain.* New York, N.Y.: W. W. Norton and Company.

5. Ibid.

6. Ibid.

7. Ibid.

8. Taylor, E. 2007. *Choices and Illusions: How Did I Get Where I Am, and How Do I Get Where I Want to Be?* Carlsbad, Calif.: Hay House, Inc.

Chapter 12

1. Richardson, V. 2009. "It's Farmers vs. Fish for California Water." *The Washington Times.* http://www.washingtontimes.com/news/2009/aug/20/its-farmers-vs-fish-for-california-water

2. Taylor, E. 2007. *Choices and Illusions: How Did I Get Where I Am, and How Do I Get Where I Want to Be?* Carlsbad, Calif.: Hay House, Inc.

Chapter 15

1. Locke, J. 1988. *Two Treatises of Government.* P. Laslett (ed.). Cambridge, UK: Cambridge University Press.

Chapter 18

1. General Assembly of the United Nations. 1948. Universal Declaration of Human Rights. **http://www.un.org/en /documents/udhr**

2. Ibid.

3. Newdow, M. 2005. "Judge Roy Moore Deserves Jail." **http://www.beliefnet.com/News/2003/08/Judge-Roy -Moore-Deserves-Jail.aspx**

4. Unknown. "Mass crimes against humanity & genocide." **http://www.religioustolerance.org/genocide0.htm**

5. Gill, K. "Pros and Cons of the Death Penalty (Capital Punishment)." *About.com.* **http://uspolitics.about.com /od/deathpenalty/i/death_penalty.htm**

6. Wikipedia. 2010. "Social Security." **http://en.wikipedia .org/wiki/Social_security**

Chapter 19

1. Ament, P. 2006. "Fascinating Facts About Joseph Swan: Inventor of the Light Bulb in 1879." **http://www .ideafinder.com/history/inventors/swan.htm**

2. Principe, L. M. 2006. *Science and Religion*. Chantilly, Va.: The Teaching Company.

3. Ibid.

4. Ibid.

5. Ibid.

6. Ibid.

7. Ibid.

8. Ibid.

9. Gabler, M. 2002. "Citizens 249, Education Establishment 0." *The Mel Gablers' Educational Research Analysts.* http://www.textbookreviews.org/index.html?content=nl_11_02.htm

10. McKinley, J. 2010. "Texas Conservatives Win Curriculum Change." *The New York Times.* http://www.nytimes.com/2010/03/13/education/13texas.html

11. Gabler, M. 2002. "Citizens 249, Education Establishment 0." *The Mel Gablers' Educational Research Analysts.* http://www.textbookreviews.org/index.html?content=nl_11_02.htm

12. Parsons, R. 2009. *Some Lies And Errors Of History (1893)*. Whitefish, Mont.: Kessinger Publishing.

13. Schweikart, L. 2009. *48 Liberal Lies About American History: (That You Probably Learned in School)*. New York, N.Y.: Sentinel Trade.

14. Unknown. 2010. "White house brass split on stimulus stats." *Politico.* http://www.politico.com/news/stories/0110/31914.html

15. Taylor, E. 2009. *Mind Programming: From Persuasion and Brainwashing to Self Help and Practical Metaphysics*. Carlsbad, Calif.: Hay House, Inc.

16. Laing, R. 1976. *The Politics of Experience*. New York, N.Y.: Ballantine Books.

Chapter 20

1. Jonas, W. B. and Crawford, C. C. 2002. *Healing, Intention and Energy Medicine*. New York, N.Y.: Churchill Livingstone.

Chapter 21

1. Gouëffic, L. 2010. *An Inconvenient Lie: Secrets in Language*. Aurora, Ontario: TTS Distributing.

2. Taylor, E. 2009. *Mind Programming: From Persuasion and Brainwashing to Self Help and Practical Metaphysics*. Carlsbad, Calif.: Hay House, Inc.

3. Gouëffic, L. 2010. *An Inconvenient Lie: Secrets in Language*. Aurora, Ontario: TTS Distributing.

4. Ibid.

5. Hudson, A. 2009. "Homeland agency pulled back extremism dictionary." *The Washington Times*. **http:// www.washingtontimes.com/news/2009/may/05 /homeland-pulled-back-extremism-dictionary**

6. Stannard, D. 1993. *American Holocaust: The Conquest of the New World*. New York, N.Y.: Oxford University Press.

7. Gergen, D. 1996. "Harvard's 'Talented Tenth.'" *U.S. News & World Report*. **http://www.usnews.com/usnews /opinion/articles/960318/archive_010008.htm**

8. Taylor, E. 2007. *Choices and Illusions: How Did I Get Where I Am, and How Do I Get Where I Want to Be?* Carlsbad, Calif.: Hay House, Inc.

9. Walsch, N. D. 1998. *The Little Soul and the Sun*. Newbury-port, Mass: Hampton Roads Publishing.

10. Laurence, J. and Perry, C. 1988. *Hypnosis, Will, and Memory: A Psycho-Legal History*. New York, N.Y.: The Guilford Press.

Chapter 23

1. Wikipedia. "Simulated Reality." **http://en.wikipedia .org/wiki/Simulated_reality#Nick_Bostrom**

2. Wikipedia. "Christopher Langton." **http://en.wikipedia .org/wiki/Christopher_Langton**

3. Bostrom, N. 2003. "Are You Living In a Computer Simulation?" *Philosophical Quarterly*: 53: 211:243–255.

4. Kaku, M. 1994. *Hyperspace*. New York, N.Y.: Oxford University Press.

5. Sheldrake, R. 1995. *The Presence of the Past: Morphic Resonance & the Habits of Nature*. Rochester, Vt.: Park Street Press.

6. Ibid.

7. Wikipedia. "Turing Completeness." **http://en.wikipedia .org/wiki/Turing_completeness**

Chapter 25

1. Lynne, D. 2005. "Life and Death Tug of War: The Whole Terri Schiavo Story." *World Net Daily*. **http://www.wnd .com/news/article.asp?ARTICLE_ID=43463**

2. Biever, B. 2010. "Giving the 'Unconscious' A Voice." *New Scientist*: 2746.

3. Ritter, M. 2010. "Study: Vegetative Brains Show Signs of Awareness." *Newsvine.com.* http://www.newsvine.com /_news/2010/02/03/3850507-study-vegetative-brains -show-signs-of-awareness

Chapter 26

1. Showalter, E. 1997. *Hystories: Hysterical Epidemics and Modern Culture.* West Sussex, UK: Columbia University Press.

2. Zimbardo, P. 2007. *The Lucifer Effect.* New York, N.Y.: Random House.

3. Wikipedia. "Murder of Kitty Genovese." http://en .wikipedia.org/wiki/Kitty_Genovese

4. Singer, S. 2008. "Video Shows Bystanders Ignoring Hit-And-Run Victim." *USA Today.* http://www.usatoday .com/news/nation/2008-06-05-1666476272_x.htm

5. Unknown. 2010. "Self-Control Is Contagious, Study Finds." *Livescience.com.* http://www.livescience.com /health/self-control-contagious-100115.html

6. Taylor, E. 2009. *Mind Programming: From Persuasion and Brainwashing to Self Help and Practical Metaphysics.* Carlsbad, Calif.: Hay House, Inc.

7. Taylor, E. 1988. *Simple Things and Simple Thoughts.* Medical Lake, Wash.: Progressive Awareness.

Appendix

1. The U.N. General Assembly, 1948. Universal Declaration of Human Rights. United Nations. http://www.un.org /en/documents/udhr

Acknowledgments

It is said, "I would give up everything to know no thing." In the play of life, at some point that may be just what we do, but until then, "I will give of myself, of my very best effort, to repay everything that has been given to me by all of you and all that is." To that end, I must acknowledge my indebtedness to All, and I hope that this work lives up to my promise.

Now, I wish also to acknowledge those special individuals who have significantly contributed to this book. To that end, I must first recognize and offer my deepest thanks to my lovely bride of more than 20 years, Ravinder, for her tireless and persistent diligence to every detail in the preparation of the final manuscript. Thank you, Suzanne Brady, for 25 years of exceptional editing. Thank you, Jessica Kelley, for your special input and the final dress given the book. Thank you, Jill Kramer and the Hay House team, for your dedication to excellence!

About the Author

Eldon Taylor is the host of the popular radio show, *Provocative Enlightenment*. He is an award-winning *New York Times* best-selling author of over 300 books, and audio or video programs. His most recent books include *Choices and Illusions, Mind Programming,* and *What Does That Mean?*

Eldon is also the inventor of the patented InnerTalk technology and the founder and President of Progressive Awareness Research, Inc. He has been featured as an expert in films, print, television, and radio. He has been called a "master of the mind" and has appeared as an expert witness on both hypnosis and subliminal communication.

More than 20 scientific studies have been conducted evaluating Eldon's technology and approach, all demonstrating its power and efficacy.

Eldon is listed in more than a dozen Who's Who publications including *Who's Who in Intellectuals* and *Who's Who in Science and Engineering.* He is a Fellow in the American Psychotherapy Association and an internationally sought-after speaker. His books and audio/video materials have been translated into more than a dozen languages and have sold millions worldwide.

Website: **www.eldontaylor.com**

To Learn More about Eldon Taylor

If you've enjoyed this book and would like to learn more about tools to help you become the person you were meant to be, visit Eldon's Website: **http://www.eldontaylor.com.**

If you're interested in gaining more control over your self-talk and your own inner beliefs, you may wish to try Eldon's patented audio technology, known as InnerTalk. Independent researchers have repeatedly proven that InnerTalk is effective at changing thoughts and thereby influencing behavior in a variety of areas affecting our daily lives.

You may download free samples of InnerTalk and find a large selection of self-improvement products by going to **http://www.innertalk.com.**

To be informed about Eldon's latest research and work and to hear about special offers on Eldon's books and audio products, please subscribe to his free e-newsletter by going to **http://www.eldontaylor.com.** You may also request a free catalog by calling 800-964-3551 or writing to Progressive Awareness Research, Inc., P.O. Box 1139, Medical Lake, WA 99022.

InnerTalk Distribution

USA
Progressive Awareness Research, Inc.
PO Box 1139
Medical Lake, WA 99022
U.S.A.
1-800-964-3551
1-509-244-6362
www.innertalk.com

UK
Vitalia Health
P. O. Box 2492
Marlow, Bucks SL7 2WW
UK
011 44 1628 898 366
www.innertalk.co.uk

Germany
Axent Verlag
Steinerne Furt 78
86167 Augsburg
Germany
011 49 821 70 5011
www.axent-verlag.de

**Malaysia/Singapore/Brunei/Australia/
New Zealand/Papua New Guinea**
InnerTalk Sdn Bhd
2–2 Jalan Pju 8/5E, Perdana Bus. Cntr.
Bandar Damansara Perdana,
47820 Petaling Jaya
Selangor, Malaysia
011 60 37 729 4745
www.innertalk-au.com
www.innertalk.co.nz
www.innertalk.com.my

Taiwan and China
Easy MindOpen
3F, No. 257, Ho-Ping East Rd. Sec. 2
Taipei, Taiwan, R.O.C
011 886 (227) 010–468(1)
www.iamone.com.tw

Distribution Inquiries

For information about distributing InnerTalk programs, please contact:

Progressive Awareness Research, Inc.
PO Box 1139
Medical Lake, WA 99022
1-800-964-3551
1-509-244-6362
www.innertalk.com

Hay House Titles of Related Interest

YOU CAN HEAL YOUR LIFE, *the movie,*
starring Louise L. Hay & Friends
(available as a 1-DVD program and an expanded 2-DVD set)
Watch the trailer at: **www.LouiseHayMovie.com**

THE SHIFT, *the movie,*
starring Dr. Wayne W. Dyer
(available as a 1-DVD program and an expanded 2-DVD set)
Watch the trailer at: **www.DyerMovie.com**

Awakening to the Secret Code of Your Mind: Your Mind's Journey to Inner Peace, by Dr. Darren R. Weissman

The Body Knows . . . How to Stay Young, by Caroline Sutherland

The Everest Principle: How to Achieve the Summit of Your Life, by Stephen C. Brewer, M.D., and Peggy Holt Wagner, M.S., L.P.C.

Messages from Spirit: The Extraordinary Power of Oracles, Omens, and Signs, by Colette Baron-Reid

Modern-Day Miracles: Miraculous Moments and Extraordinary Stories from People All Over the World Whose Lives Have Been Touched by Louise L. Hay, by Louise L. Hay & Friends

The Mother of Invention: The Legacy of Barbara Marx Hubbard and the Future of YOU, by Neale Donald Walsch

Simply . . . EMPOWERED! Discover How to Create and Sustain Success in Every Area of Your Life, by Crystal Andrus

Soul on Fire, by Peter Calhoun

Truth Heals: *What You Hide Can Hurt You,* by Deborah King

Truth, Triumph, and Transformation: *Sorting Out the Fact from Fiction in Universal Law,* by Sandra Anne Taylor

Your Destiny Switch: *Master Your Key Emotions, and Attract the Life of Your Dreams!* by Peggy McColl

All of the above are available at your local bookstore, or may be ordered by contacting Hay House (see next page).

We hope you enjoyed this Hay House book. If you'd like to receive our online catalog featuring additional information on Hay House books and products, or if you'd like to find out more about the Hay Foundation, please contact:

Hay House, Inc., P.O. Box 5100, Carlsbad, CA 92018-5100
(760) 431-7695 or (800) 654-5126
(760) 431-6948 (fax) or (800) 650-5115 (fax)
www.hayhouse.com® • **www.hayfoundation.org**

Published and distributed in Australia by:
Hay House Australia Pty. Ltd., 18/36 Ralph St., Alexandria NSW 2015
Phone: 612-9669-4299 • *Fax:* 612-9669-4144 • www.hayhouse.com.au

Published and distributed in the United Kingdom by:
Hay House UK, Ltd., 292B Kensal Rd., London W10 5BE • *Phone:*
44-20-8962-1230 • *Fax:* 44-20-8962-1239 • www.hayhouse.co.uk

Published and distributed in the Republic of South Africa by:
Hay House SA (Pty), Ltd., P.O. Box 990, Witkoppen 2068
Phone/Fax: 27-11-467-8904 • www.hayhouse.co.za

Published in India by: Hay House Publishers India, Muskaan
Complex, Plot No. 3, B-2, Vasant Kunj, New Delhi 110 070 • *Phone:*
91-11-4176-1620 • *Fax:* 91-11-4176-1630 • www.hayhouse.co.in

Distributed in Canada by:
Raincoast, 9050 Shaughnessy St., Vancouver, B.C. V6P 6E5
Phone: (604) 323-7100 • *Fax:* (604) 323-2600 • www.raincoast.com

Take Your Soul on a Vacation

Visit **www.HealYourLife.com®** to regroup, recharge,
and reconnect with your own magnificence.
Featuring blogs, mind-body-spirit news, and life-changing
wisdom from Louise Hay and friends.

Visit **www.HealYourLife.com** today!

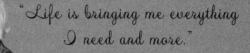